The Legacy Continues...

*Stories of Precious Blood Sisters
Continuing the Legacy
of
Mother Maria Anna Brunner*

CPPS Biographies Project
Volume II

Sisters of the Precious Blood
Dayton, Ohio

WovenWord Press

The Legacy Continues. . .
Sisters of the Precious Blood
WovenWord Press
811 Mapleton Avenue
Boulder, Colorado
80304
Copyright © 2001

ISBN 0967842832

Dedication

To all Sisters of the Precious Blood
living and laboring today
to share the power of Jesus' Precious Blood
with those in need
by meeting the challenges of each day
with
unbounded FAITH in God's truth,
confident HOPE in God's mercy,
and
passionate LOVE for God
and all God's creatures.

Acknowledgments

This second volume in the Biographies Project continues telling stories of Sisters of the Precious Blood who lived out the legacy of their foundress, Mother Maria Anna Brunner. We are grateful to sisters, former students, families, friends and colleagues who have contributed their memories, making this book possible.

Special thanks to:

❖ Sister Maryann Bremke, President of the Congregation, for her enthusiastic encouragement of this project.

❖ Sister Noreen Jutte, Congregational Archivist, for access to archival material and for copying services.

❖ Sisters Mary Louise Barhorst, Marie Bax, Virgine Elking Berenice Janszen, and Eileen Monnin for their careful reading of the manuscripts and for their helpful suggestions.

❖ All the sisters and others who shared memories of sisters, making it possible to bring them to life once again.

❖ All who have affirmed us and encouraged us in this project.

❖ Sheila Durkin Dierks and Vicki McVey of WovenWord Press for their help and patience in guiding the production of this book.

CPPS Biographies Project
Volume II

Project Director	Helen Weber CPPS
Writers	Cordelia Gast CPPS
	Eleanor McNally CPPS
	Helen Weber CPPS
Editor	Anne Agnew CPPS
Researcher	Canice Werner CPPS
Historian	Cordelia Gast CPPS

We are pleased to present Volume II of the CPPS Biographies Project. This has been a cooperative effort of a large number of persons. We are grateful to all who have contributed to this project in any way.

Volume I has been received with enthusiasm by a variety of our publics, and many have urged us to continue the series. With a deepening appreciation for the Sisters of the Precious Blood who have preceded us, we plan at least one additional volume. This will be published in June, 2002.

Unfortunately, we find ourselves limited by a paucity of records and documents. Because of this, we are unable to write about many of our outstanding sisters. Over the years thousands of women have dedicated their lives to follow the charism of Jesus' Precious Blood, as modeled by Maria Anna Brunner. In the stories of the sisters in Volumes I, II and III, may each sister find some part of her own story of love and fidelity.

Contents

Volume II

Preface

Volume II of the CPPS Biographies Project continues the stories of sisters who exemplified the charism of the Precious Blood of Jesus as followers of Mother Maria Anna Brunner. This book tells of sisters who served in a variety of ministries. Though one tale deals primarily with one sister, the other two combine the lives of several sisters because they were so intertwined.

"Where Two or Three Are Gathered . . ." was written by Cordelia Gast CPPS and Helen Weber CPPS. As a niece of Margaret Gast CPPS, one of the three sisters featured in this story, Cordelia provided a unique perspective by sharing intimate information of her talented aunt.

"Crimsoned Sands" was written by Eleanor McNally CPPS. Her firsthand knowledge of the Congregation's history in Arizona came from her experience both as a student and a teacher at St. Mary's High School, and later as Regional Director of the Western Region of the Congregation.

"I Come to Do Your Will," written by Helen Weber CPPS, was based largely upon personal writings of Sister Ludgeria Bellinghausen CPPS, the subject of this story, and those of persons who appreciated her dedication and versatility.

As in Volume I, we have not used the title "Sister" after the initial introduction, except in the case of Mother Superiors and others in authority. For increased clarity when quoting from contemporary writings, minor adjustments in spelling and grammar have been made. We have used italics for longer quotations taken from writings by the subjects.

Unfortunately, many of the sources used were anonymous. Because they conveyed the flavor of the person or the situation, we have, in many cases, used quotations from these sources without attribution.

Where Two or Three Are Gathered. . .

by

Cordelia Gast CPPS
and
Helen Weber CPPS

Stories of
Margaret Gast CPPS
Jovita Thalheimer CPPS
Arnolda (Helena) Nietfield CPPS

Prologue

The May sunshine streamed through the large east windows, brightening and warming the room where three women were busily sewing. A gentle serenity seemed to hover over them and the piles of work before them. Only the soft purr of the sewing machine, the clipping of the scissors and the snap of threads broke the silence.

These three women, Sisters of the Precious Blood of Dayton, Ohio, considered it a great privilege to spend their lives sewing for their sisters. But today's task was even more special. They were beginning to prepare new clothing for the young women who were about to dedicate their lives to God by taking vows of poverty, chastity and obedience. In the spring of each year, the sisters put aside all other mending and sewing to devote full time to this project. It gave them great delight to clothe and supply each young sister with all she would need to begin her ministry.

Sister Margaret Gast, the sister in charge of the sewing room, was carefully cutting new habits. The large bolt of black serge was on a specially designed pole from which material could easily be unrolled onto the large cutting table. She placed her well-worn patterns on the material and checked once again the careful measurements she had taken. Cautiously, with little or no waste of cloth, she cut the wool to the correct size needed.

Across the room, Sister Jovita Thalheimer sat at her sewing machine, somehow making the difficult stitching of black on black of the circular guimpe look easy. Her steady hand and practiced eye made meticulous and exact stitches. Each newly professed sister would be wearing this part of the habit for the first time, and Jovita wanted each one to be perfect.

Nearby, Sister Arnolda Nietfeld labored at her sewing machine diligently making white Roman collars. The stitching had to be precise to give the collar body and distinction. Each young sister would need several of these.

The quiet of the room was broken by the ringing of the "hour bell" in the chapel tower across the courtyard. Ten minutes before the beginning of each hour, the bell summoned the next group of sisters to chapel to pray before the Blessed Sacrament. Throughout the house, wherever they might be, sisters stopped what they were doing to join in this prayer. Margaret, Jovita and Arnolda paused in their work to pray together: "Praised and Blest be the Sacred Heart and the Precious Blood of Jesus in the most Holy Sacrament of the Altar. O Lord, in union with that Divine intention wherewith Thou on earth didst praise God, I offer Thee this hour of adoration."

This short invocation reminded the sisters that their primary mission was the worship of God present in the Blessed Sacrament, rather than sewing, teaching, nursing, or whatever their assignment might be. Finishing the prayer, the three sisters returned to the work they had been doing for many years. Working quietly and unseen, they served their sisters directly by making and maintaining the sisters' clothing as perfectly as possible. Experiencing peace and contentment in this humble task, they were extraordinary persons doing very ordinary things day after day with great love. Here are their stories.

Sister Margaret Gast

Her Ancestry

"Papa! Come quickly. We can see land!" shouted ten-year-old Piere Gast. With his father, André, and older brother, Mathias, he watched with fascination as their ship drew near to shore. They had emigrated to America from their home in the lovely Alpine village of Ligsdorf, France. As their ship moved up Chesapeake Bay to the city of Baltimore, Maryland, the boys' eyes eagerly surveyed the sights of this strange new country. The year was 1828.

Lingering in Baltimore no longer than necessary, André Gast and his sons moved on to Cincinnati via the Ohio River. From Cincinnati they took the pioneer route 120 miles north to what is now Mercer County, Ohio. Happy to arrive at the land made available to them, they built a log cabin in a wooded clearing called St. John's. There, father and sons established themselves as a family and contributed to the stability and growth of the new settlement.

André Gast, a shop keeper, had married Therese Bendi in France in 1808, and together they had eight children. There is no record of his wife or the couple's six other children coming to America. A genealogical record shows that Therese died in 1856 in Ligsdorf.

With the completion in 1845 of the Miami-Erie Canal between Cincinnati and Toledo, an increasing number of travelers and traders began coming into and through Mercer County. Taking advantage of this traffic, the Gast family opened their new brick home, the "Gast House," as a part-time hotel and place where travelers could take their meals.

Their home was also available for other needed services in the pioneer community. Liwät Böke, a chronicler of life in early St. John's, writes that before the first log church was built, "once or at most twice a month, there is a Mass on Sunday at St. John's. We assemble at the Gast's house. . . . Other Sundays we go there about 11:30 in the morning to pray."

André Gast's sons, Mathias and Piere, grew up and married, and some of their descendants moved to Cincinnati or to Chicago. However, Mathias's son, John Henry, and his wife, Catherine Desch, stayed at St. John's, by then known as Maria Stein. There, John and the twins, Andrew and Mary, were born. Later, this family moved to Celina where Catherine gave birth to six more children. One of these, Mathilda, born in 1872, was to become Sister Mary Margaret Gast, a Sister of the Precious Blood.

Her childhood

An amusing family story from that period tells of the efforts of five-year-old Andrew to care for his baby sister, Mathilda. This was no fun for a little boy who really wanted a dog, not a baby sister. One day he put his little sister into his wagon and trotted across the street to his friend who had a dog, but wanted a baby sister. What was more natural than to trade? Both boys were happy until Andrew arrived home, and his mother asked, "Where is your baby sister?"

Baby Mathilda was returned home and grew up a healthy child. She started first grade in 1886 at Immaculate Conception Parish School located across the street from her home. The Sisters of the Precious Blood had come from Maria Stein, some 14 miles away, to begin the school in Celina in 1879. A new school was built in 1889, and the Gast children completed their education with the sisters.

After she concluded her elementary education, Mathilda helped in whatever ways she could to provide for the family. There were nine children in all; two boys had died when they were small. Their father ran a small grocery store, but the income from it was insufficient for the family's needs. Desiring to help, Mathilda learned to sew from her brother, Andrew, who had completed an apprenticeship with a local tailor and started his own business. Working with her brother, she soon became a skilled tailor.

Since the Gast family lived close to the church, they often helped there when needed. One day, while working in the rectory, Mathilda picked up a book on the spiritual life. As she was reading, she felt God calling her to be a religious. At that very time, the novices at Maria Stein were praying that God would direct their way a young woman who could be a seamstress. Their prayers were answered when Mathilda Gast, then 29 years old, applied for admittance into the Congregation on December 4, 1909.

Early Religious Life

Mathilda adapted easily to religious life, and the postulancy and novitiate passed quickly. She revered and respected Sister Regula Dann, the novice mistress. There is evidence that the feelings between this somewhat older, more mature novice and the novice mistress were reciprocal, since they remained life-long friends. Upon reception as a novice, Mathilda Gast received the name of Sister Mary Margaret.

As Margaret's profession date grew nearer, a disagreement was brewing between Margaret's superiors. Sister Regula wanted Margaret to be assigned to the sewing room at Maria Stein. Sister Victoria Drees, directress of schools, wanted her to become a teacher. Somehow the problem was resolved, for Margaret made her profession at the appointed time, August 15, 1913. She received the assignment to teach at St. Mary School in Dayton, Ohio.

After teaching two years at St. Mary's, Margaret was sent to St. Joseph School in Wapakoneta, Ohio. There she taught seventh grade for three years enjoying the classroom very much. Margaret seemed destined to be a teacher.

While Margaret was teaching in Wapakoneta, a world-wide epidemic of Spanish influenza raged. Public health officials estimated that there were over twenty million deaths across the globe. Schools and churches were closed. Margaret returned from Wapakoneta to the Maria Stein Convent, and there learned that her own family was stricken. As soon as she was able, she traveled to Celina to be of assistance. The dreaded disease claimed the lives of her mother, her pregnant sister who had been married less than a year, and two of her nephews. Few families were left unscathed by this tragedy.

While Margaret was in Celina, she visited her brother, Andrew, in his tailor shop. He had married in 1915 and had one daughter, Mary, who was then two-years-old. Visiting her brother's home, Margaret observed the tiny girl playing with a toy car. When someone asked the child where the car was going, she replied brightly, "To Dayton." Since the family knew no one in Dayton, they were puzzled by the answer. Twelve years later, when little Mary entered the Sisters of the Precious Blood in Dayton, Margaret looked back on this incident as prophetic. Her niece, Mary, became Sister Mary Cordelia Gast.

When the severity of the flu lessened, Margaret returned to Wapakoneta for the remainder of the school year. In the summer of 1919, the sister in charge of sewing habits at Maria Stein became ill. Margaret had been helping with sewing during her free time; now she was asked to take over the main duties of the sewing room. Sister Regula's wish years before was being fulfilled. Thus, Margaret began her life-long service of sewing for the Congregation—a work that would continue for the next 36 years.

Margaret bore the responsibility for transferring the sewing room from Maria Stein to Salem Heights.

For the first five years, Margaret basically worked alone in the sewing room. Sister teachers helped her during the summer, and retired sisters assisted with the mending. However, the major tasks of habit-making were Margaret's charge. With her skill in tailoring, the habit took on a different look as it was carefully made for each person with precise and exact fitting. Since Margaret was skilled in working with wool, the Sunday habits of the sisters were made of black serge. As the Congregation grew, so did the demands on Margaret's sewing room. Keeping the sisters properly outfitted became much more than one person could do.

In 1923 the Sisters of the Precious Blood relocated their motherhouse to Salem Heights, northwest of Dayton. In the new building, the third-floor sewing room was spacious, and since its large windows faced east, it was light and airy.

Margaret brought along with her much of the equipment she had used at Maria Stein—including a unique iron she used for pressing. Every morning after breakfast, Margaret placed lighted charcoal into the iron, and the heated iron was used all day. Even later, when electric irons became easily available, Margaret preferred the iron-box and continued to use it for many years.

Margaret struggled to keep up with the ever-increasing clothing needs of the Congregation. Eventually, it became evident that another trained seamstress was needed. God provided, and a 27-year-old woman from Minster, Ohio applied for membership in the Congregation.

Sister Jovita Thalheimer

Marian Thalheimer was born in 1897 in Lima, Ohio. She and her brother were left motherless at a very young age and were cared for by the Sisters of the Precious Blood in the orphanage in Minister. When young Marian left the boarding school, she was apprenticed to a seamstress in the town and spent the next ten years studying the trade. She learned how to use the sewing machine, make new garments, do alterations and mend.

As Marian grew older and became independent, she became aware of another need in her life. After praying about it, she talked with the sisters about the spiritual hunger she was experiencing. Gradually, she came to a realization that God was calling her to religious life. Since the Sisters of the Precious Blood had been so much a part of her life, at 27 years of age she sought admission to the Congregation.

Mother Agreda Sperber accepted Marian as a postulant at Salem Heights Convent in September, 1924. It was evident to all that Sister Mary Jovita, the name she received at her investiture, would be assigned after profession to the general sewing room at Salem Heights. There she would stay for the next fifty years.

Undoubtedly, Margaret welcomed such an able assistant. To the skills that Jovita already possessed, Margaret added the fine points of tailoring. The two sisters worked together in the sewing room for thirty years. While Margaret took care of the general management of the department and the cutting of new habits, Jovita assumed responsibility for sewing in the black goods section. Many years later, she commented that her eyes became very used to sewing black on black.

Jovita was a quiet and unassuming woman whose life was centered on her day and night hours of adoration and on her service to the sisters. Her demeanor always exuded a gentle peacefulness. She was also responsible for reading at table during meals and for 15 minutes of spiritual reading in chapel before supper. For many years, her resonant voice echoed through the chapel each evening as she read the necrology and the points for meditation. Her strong, clear voice never needed amplification by a microphone.

Sister Helena Nietfeld

A Tiny Orphan

Snow was falling softly on that cold November day in 1911 as the train pulled into the station in Fort Recovery, Ohio. A ten-year-old girl gazed expectantly out of the train window. Maybe in this town she would be chosen to be someone's little girl.

Helena Reilly had been traveling on the train for about a week. She was one of a group of children from an orphanage in New York City being taken to small towns in the rural Midwest. The only home she had ever known was the orphanage run by the Sisters of Charity. She did not even remember her own parents. The sisters told her that her mother and father had brought her to the orphanage when she was a small child because they were unable to care for her. She knew that her parents, the O'Reillys, had come from Ireland as emigrants shortly before she was born. They were poor and had not been able to make enough money to care for their baby. The journey had been difficult, and they were in poor health. With heavy hearts they left their baby girl with the sisters.

Over the years, when little Helena asked the sisters about her family, she was urged to forget them. The sisters assured her that she would always be taken care of as a member of the orphanage family. By 1911 orphanages in large eastern cities had become overcrowded because many children were in situations similar to Helena's. Hundreds of other boys and girls were much worse off, having no home or parents, and were forced to live on the streets and scavenge for food.

About fifty years before this time, the Children's Aid Society, following the inspiration of Charles Loring Brace, addressed the issue of street urchins by taking trainloads of them to the Midwest and Western parts of the country. Mr. Brace believed that rural life with a good farming family was the only salvation for these children. For many years Catholic orphanages tried to care for the many children thrust upon them. Eventually, they also joined the "Orphan Trains" to help children find good homes, making every effort to place Catholic children with Catholic families.

New Parents

The matron traveling on the train with the children came to little Helena to tell her it was time to get off the train. The little girl brushed her naturally curly hair from her face and donned her new coat, checking to make sure her birth and baptismal certificates were still sewed into its lining. Taking a deep breath, she picked up her cardboard suitcase containing all her belongings and stepped from the train onto the platform.

The children were taken to a nearby building where the people of the area had gathered to make their choices. Helena hoped that she might be chosen even though she had been passed over several times before, because most of the farmers were looking for boys who could help with chores on their farms. Trying not to be too optimistic so she wouldn't be disappointed again, Helena stood before the crowd and waited patiently.

Soon a very tall man and his wife approached Helena. The woman smiled at her with tears in her eyes. Slowly, a shy grin spread over Helena's face. The woman winked at her, and the little girl responded with a big smile and a bright twinkle in her clear blue eyes. Without hesitation, the woman said "Yes, this is the child we want."

Things happened very quickly after that. The kindly couple took Helena to those in charge of the adoption process. While the man took care of the paper work, his wife gently put her arm around Helena who at first tensed up at the touch of this stranger. Seeing the kind face of the woman, however, the little girl decided to try to trust her even as she had learned to trust the sisters at the orphanage.

After arrangements were completed, the couple took the little girl to their horse and buggy for the last lap of the trip to her new home on a farm outside of Cranberry Prairie, Ohio. Helena giggled to herself when she heard the name of the town. During the 15-mile trip, Catherine Nietfeld introduced herself and her husband, Joseph, and told the child that they had a son, John, who would be her new brother. They also confided that at one time they had a little girl about the same age as Helena, but she had died sometime before. Catherine told Helena that she would now be loved as much as their own daughter had been.

A New Name

Helena Reilly, the "O" had been dropped in the orphanage, became Helen Nietfeld and was enrolled in a one-room school. There is no record of how she made the adjustments from New York City to Cranberry Prairie, from a big city to a farming community, from an orphanage to a small family, from a large school to a one-room school, or from her Irish heritage to a family with strong German customs. However, those who knew her in later life as a happy, well-adjusted person could only conclude that the Nietfeld family had supplied young Helen with the love necessary for her to develop into a self-confident woman.

What Helen did after she left school—probably at about age 13—is unknown. At 25 she entered religious life at the new Motherhouse of the Sisters of the Precious Blood in

Dayton. Probably, she followed the custom of "working out" prevalent in those days for young unmarried rural women. Traditionally, young women assisted neighboring families when new babies were born, or when women needed help in caring for an elderly family member.

Helen began her religious life on November 15, 1926. She received the name of Sister Mary Arnolda at investiture. After her profession, she was assigned to work under Sister Margaret in the sewing room at Salem Heights where she stayed for the next 25 years, from 1929 to 1954.

Changing Habits

By the time Margaret set up the sewing room in the new Motherhouse, all the sisters were clothed alike in a religious habit. This had not always been the case. *Not with Silver or Gold*, the Congregational history, says:

> No habit peculiar to the institute was adopted during the lifetime of the foundress nor for some years afterward. The dress of the earliest members, modest in cut and black in color, differed little in style from the native Swiss garb (p. 63).

Postulants entering after the Congregation's move to the United States in 1844 were told to bring three simple, modest black dresses. Within a short time, some uniform clothing seems to have existed, especially for teaching sisters. Again, quoting from the Congregational history:

> Their garments were for the most part home-spun; their shoes and hose were their own manufacture. By this time [1850s] a uniform religious habit had been adopted. It was made of poor material, severely black, with a veil 'similar to those worn by American women in mourning' (p. 151).

When the sisters came under the jurisdiction of the Archbishop of Cincinnati in 1888, they were encouraged to wear more professional clothing. A tailored black habit with a black veil was adopted for all professed sisters. The postulants wore a simple black dress with a brown bonnet; the novices dressed in similar fashion, with a black bonnet. Beginning in 1925 the novices received a white veil at investiture.

The severe blackness of the habit was broken slightly in 1906 when white piping was added to the collar. Five years later, Archbishop Henry Moeller suggested that the sisters consider making the whole collar white. He wrote, "A little white added to the somber dark color of the habit would give it an air of cheerfulness, especially necessary in the school-room." The Congregation complied with his suggestion, but the habit did not undergo further changes until 15 years later.

When Margaret assumed responsibility for the sewing department in 1919, most of the sewing involved black material. It would not be until 1926 that Mother Agreda changed the headgear to consist of a white skull cap and a white veil frame under a black veil. The white linen around the sisters' faces created a much less severe appearance.

A Touch of Red

Again an Archbishop made suggestions to the Congregation about the sisters' clothing. In 1928 Archbishop John T. McNicholas suggested that a bit of red be added to the habit to symbolize the Precious Blood. Complying with his suggestion, a red cincture was substituted for the black belt, and a red cross string replaced the black one. No additional changes were made in the habit for the next 30 years.

Each time decisions were made regarding the habit, the sewing department was expected to figure out what needed to be done. Margaret seemed to take these changes in stride. She designed the white headgear, and all the sisters were able to change within a short time. But the addition of the red cord and cincture presented a challenge that could not be solved with a needle and thread. What could she do? Many years earlier at St. Mary's, Dayton, Margaret had lived with Sister Mary Theonilla Thom, a multi-talented woman known for

*A young Arnolda (Helena) models
the finely tailored habit the sisters
wore from 1928 to 1955.*

her artistic and creative genius. Margaret approached Theonilla with the problem of the cincture and the red cord.

Theonilla studied the matter and decided that the cincture needed to be made of tightly woven red yarn. To create about 600 cinctures by hand would take months and would require the services of many sisters to twist the yarn. This method, she realized, would result in an uneven product. To solve this dilemma, she invented a machine similar to those farmers used to make rope. Using her machine, a few sisters could supply the whole Congregation in a short period of time. The cinctures and the cords produced in this way were even and tightly woven. Each year a few sisters could easily make what was needed. Theonilla's invention continued to be used long after Theonilla was unable to do the job herself.

All clothing for the sisters—from undergarments to aprons and outer cloaks—was made in the sewing room. Margaret designed the garments, made patterns to fit various sizes, cut the cloth and did some of the sewing. She ordered the cloth, calculating how much would be needed each year, and she directed the work of her assistants. For all this, she kept exact records.

When a sister needed a new item of clothing, she went to Margaret to get measured. The seamstress kept each sister's measurements, along with the dates that clothes were requested. Margaret knew exactly how long each sister's clothes lasted. She was heard to remark that she had "rather intimate knowledge of every sister."

The Spirit of the Sewing Room

Throughout her life, Margaret looked upon daily happenings as evidence of God's will leading to salvation. Her needle became her "key to heaven." She borrowed this idea from a Franciscan lay brother who was the tailor for his brothers. On his deathbed, he asked for his needle and addressed it thus:

> Many years, old friend, we've tailored
> Every stitch I've made with thee
> was for God's dear glory taken
> for the blest eternity.

Margaret always viewed her work as God's work. Cordelia, her niece, tells about an experience she had with her aunt:

> Margaret once instructed me when I was helping out in the sewing room, 'Always cut the thread on the sewing machine as close as you conveniently can. Otherwise these wasted pieces will be knotted together and form a rope to hold you in purgatory.' This idea may not sound too uplifting today, but it did alert me to the way Margaret made the practice of the consciousness of God's presence in the least detail of her life.

That Margaret lived in the presence of God was easily discernible in the conversations she often had with sisters whose clothing she was fitting. One sister remembers:

> When getting measured for a new habit, Sister Margaret gave various tidbits of practical wisdom, at times so heart warming and inspirational that they clung to you long after the clothes you ordered were threadbare.

16

Another added:

> When being measured for clothes, a real sense of love for the person emanated from Sister Margaret. You gained an appreciation of what it meant to be called to religious life by the way she lived her life.

Margaret (on left) was always very
proud of her niece, Cordelia.

One sister kept for years, and often repeated, a little prayer Margaret had written on a scrap of paper and carefully tucked in with some clothing: "O Jesus, make me a religious according to your own Heart."

There were also lighter moments in Margaret's sewing room. Each year the novices were sent to Margaret to be measured for their new profession habits. Most of the habits were made of wool serge and tailored with pleats in the back from the waist to the shoulders. Because of the intense heat in Arizona, sisters being assigned there received habits made of lighter weight and without the upper pleats.

Novices naturally were curious about where they were being sent for their first mission. They often tried to reach up behind their backs to check if there were pleats above the waist. Margaret, aware of this little tactic, made sure that they never saw the back of the habit as they were being fitted. If a novice slipped her hand around, Margaret would push it away, telling her that all she needed to do was remain trusting and obedient. What delight she and her staff must have had in being able to keep the curious novices guessing!

Margaret kept meticulous files on each sister. She knew when it was time for each one to have new clothing. She would send word to a sister needing a new habit to come to the sewing room during the annual retreat. From time to time there were sisters who, for whatever reason, needed additional clothing. Sister Norma Osterloh tells the following story: During her second year after novitiate, she couldn't understand why the seams in her habit kept breaking, so she went to Margaret and told her. Margaret checked her measurements and said to Norma, "Child, you are no longer a child, but you are now a woman," and she made a new habit for Norma with her new measurements. No sister was ever intimidated by Margaret, and all were treated with dignity and respect in responding to their clothing requests.

Jovita brought a quiet humor to her work. Always willing to do what was asked of her, she is remembered as a person who spoke little and smiled much. Her interior life of continual prayer was evident in her reserved but pleasant manner.

Arnolda's delightfully cheerful personality added some lightness to the workplace. Her clever comments coming from her Irish wit often broke the tension of the day. Her soft-spoken words and generous smile made her a valued co-worker.

All three of these sisters treasured their regular hours of prayer before the Blessed Sacrament, drawing their strength for their work from these hours of contemplation.

The Gray Habit

After a long and difficult Congregational debate at the 1954 Assembly, the Sisters of the Precious Blood decided to change from a black habit to one of light gray. While the black habit had been made of heavy wool serge, the new gray ones were made of a light-weight synthetic material. The decision to change was based on the need to have lighter clothing that could easily be washed. Still, many sisters, who considered a 100-year history of wearing the black habit a sacred tradition,

Wearing the newly-designed gray habit, Helena left Salem Heights to serve at the Chancery in Cincinnati.

found this decision very hard to accept.

Margaret, who had spent most of her life making the tailored black serge habits, had considerable difficulty adjusting to the change. She was 74 years old and ready to retire. Although she moved to Lourdes Hall, the Congregation's infirmary, she was not idle. She continued to sew and mend clothing for the retired sisters.

Jovita stayed on in the sewing room where she had worked with black material for so many years. She said her eyes were accustomed to it, and she didn't want to change to work on gray. Besides hemming the long veils, Jovita spent a considerable amount of time converting the long black cloaks into coats that could be worn over the new habits. The sisters had requested a coat rather than the long cloak to give them more freedom of movement, especially when driving. This required that Jovita design coats with sleeves that could accommodate the cape of the habit. The product of her imaginative thinking was an outer garment that was a cross between a cloak and a coat. Almost single-handedly, she transformed the sisters' cloaks into new coats.

Arnolda left the sewing room with the advent of the gray habits. By then most of the sisters purchased their own undergarments and were expected to do their own mending. The gray habits required less skill to make, and most of the mission houses had electric sewing machines. Novitiate training now included learning to sew and to care for one's own clothing.

On August 22, 1955, all Sisters of the Precious Blood donned the new gray habit simultaneously wherever they were. This day was preceded by a year of intensive work. About 700 sisters and novices needed new gray habits—far too many for any one person or one department to produce. This project required mobilization of all sisters able to run a sewing machine, or to learn to do so. Sister Marcella Ensman was called upon to manage this huge undertaking. It was a time of feverish activity.

The sisters wore the gray habit for a little over 10 years, after which time the habit was made optional by the Assembly of 1966. Gradually, most of the sisters began to wear simple and easy-to-care-for secular clothing.

Margaret's Final Days

Margaret lived in Lourdes Hall for about 10 years after she retired as manager of the sewing room. Throughout this time, she retained her quiet dignity and her contemplative nature. For as long as she was able, she helped the retired sisters by mending their clothes.

Sister Margaret Rigdon relates that when she was a nurse in Lourdes Hall, one of her duties was to take medicine to the sisters. Although Margaret did not take any medicine at that time, she would always stand by her door for a chance to give the salutation, "Praised be Jesus Christ." This was similar to her custom, when she was still active, of walking to the door of the sewing room with a sister who was leaving, taking holy water, and signing her forehead saying "May Jesus and Mary bless you, and may the holy angels watch over you." Margaret had a way of reminding sisters that their purpose in life was to praise the Lord God through their work and way of life.

Gradually Margaret's hearing lessened and her sight dimmed. She became seriously ill with arterial sclerosis and died peacefully on August 25, 1964. She was 84 years of age, having spent 54 years in religious life, and 35 years in direct service to her sisters.

Jovita's Later Years

Jovita lived quietly in the presence of the Lord. Few knew her beyond her work in the sewing room and her special care for the cats who kept mice from invading Salem Heights. After each meal she could be seen carrying leftovers from the kitchen to feed them. She loved all of creation and treated every part of it with gentle care.

Jovita's yearly obedience from 1927 through 1968 read "Sewing Room, Salem Heights." In addition to her assignment in the sewing department, she spent hours in adoration before the Blessed Sacrament. In 1968 she retired from the sewing room but continued both her day and night hours of adoration as long as she was physically able.

Jovita lived a humble and unassuming life. Few were permitted an insight into the woman she was and her closeness to God. During the 70s, the Congregation initiated the custom of having one of the retired sisters join in the ministry of an active sister through prayer. Jovita chose to pray for Sister Anne Agnew who kept many of the notes Jovita wrote over the years. Excerpts from these provide a glimpse into Jovita's keen sense of humor and deep spirituality. Most of the notes are undated, but they range from 1975 to 1985 when she was between 78 and 88 years of age.

When she retired, her room became a combination bedroom and sewing room. She kept her faithful sewing machine so that she could still help the sisters in the care of their clothes. She wrote:

> *I am still sewing all odds and ends. Retailing shirts, lining coats, hemming veils, darning socks and patching—even mop sticks and anything that our old sisters hold as practicing poverty. I am the busybody that keeps our old sisters from getting too hole-y. They don't mind how many patches it takes to cover the holes, just so they get them back?? hole-y poverty.*

21

Jovita's birthday was April 1—April Fools' Day. Throughout her life she had great fun calling herself an April Fool. In 1975 she wrote:

> *I celebrated my birthday. April Fool people can't forget. My 78 years have passed quickly; and with the Lord's help, I am still able to help myself and also others with a stitch in time to prevent their hol-e-ness.*

As her health deteriorated, Jovita could look at herself and the frailty of the human body with her customary good humor:

> *I stumbled in July and fell on my face and got a bump on the nose which will leave a lump on my beak for the rest of my days.*

> *You asked me if it were possible for me to come to Cincy. I think it best for me to stay at home. I can't trust my stompers from one day to another. . . . I'm soon 84 so I'm close to the end. Otherwise I'm deaf and not much company, you would get hoarse shouting.*

> *I am still a member of the Holy Rollers, going to the dining room on wheels! My combination sewing room and bedroom is just outside the Chapel, quite convenient, such a short distance, I can walk and, best of all, run the sewing machine, never out of work.*

> *I've had a blood clot and an open leg four times in the right leg, and the doctor tells me that it's going to go on like that to the end?? I take him at his word, but there is Someone higher up who is taking care of that business.*

> *I don't know if you will be able to read this letter, the screw came out of my glasses this morning, and I couldn't use my book to read in Chapel and maybe the singing went better without me???*

Jovita often commented on nature, how she appreciated the changing seasons and what beauty each one brought. In

*Jovita's impish smile greeted all who
visited her in her combination
sewing/bedroom.*

this note, after she complains about wasps getting into the
convent, she says:

> . . . *we can find more friendly neighbors. The birds take a
> sip of water and raise their heads toward heaven to thank
> the Dear God for all His blessings, for every day is a day of
> Beauty. . . .*

Many of the notes to Anne contain encouragement and
admonitions but also depict Jovita's spirituality:

> *Our Chapel was beautiful for Christmas, a small
> sanctuary is easy to fill and decorate and with our large
> Monstrance resting on the altar, it is a joy to come and
> pray. May Jesus Christ be Praised!*

> *I hope you found your job more interesting . . . and all the
> opportunities to use the energy and love that you can
> spend among the poor and needy for the greater Honor and*

Glory of God. I read we would receive greater favors if we would ask. Our loving Father will not be outdone in generosity. He holds us in the palm of His hand and remains with us day and night.

Our Feast of the Precious Blood is with us and we will make it a day of prayer and Thanksgiving for the graces we receive through the Precious Blood. God has been good to us. We have the Blessed Sacrament always with us, day and night, and have the great privilege of spending day and night hours of adoration.

One last amusing note in light of this book:

Thank you for your notebook. I will see by the end of the year how many calamities I took in or luckily missed!! Often doing the wrong thing at the right time. My biography will not look good in print. My good Guardian Angel will see to it that it will never be published.

Jovita died peacefully on February 6, 1988 at the age of ninety.

Helena's Later Years

With the changing of habits from black to gray in 1954, the need for the crew in the sewing room diminished. Arnolda received her first assignment different from all the others she had received since profession. This time it did not say "Sewing room, Salem Heights." For the first time in 25 years, Arnolda was told to leave Salem Heights. She was assigned to the Chancery in Cincinnati, but the work she was to do there was the same. Now she sewed and mended for the Archbishop and the clergy staff rather than for the sisters. Her gentle and good-natured presence brought joy to the sisters with whom she lived and to the people she served.

There are few records of Arnolda's years at the Chancery. A story told about her by Sister Berenice Janszen, however, shows that her life was not all work and no play. During the summers in the 1960s, the Glenmary nuns invited all sisters in Cincinnati to share the swimming pool at their convent. Arnolda took advantage of this opportunity as often as possible. Berenice recalls the many happy hours she spent with her in the pool, enjoying the sun, sky and water and "talking about everything under the sun."

In 1967, after 13 years at the Chancery, she was transferred to St. Peter in Chains Cathedral in Cincinnati. Her assignments included sewing for the priests, assisting with housekeeping chores and helping to serve the priests in their dining room.

*Seen here wearing a modified habit and
veil, Helena adapted easily to changes in
community garb.*

At this time Arnolda returned to her baptismal name, a permission granted by the Assembly of 1966. When the sisters in New York City took in Helena O'Reilly in 1901, they dropped the O from her last name. Later, when the Nietfelds adopted her, they dropped the "a" from her first name and called her Helen. Now, though she took back her baptismal name of Helena, she never went back to the surname of her birth parents. The Nietfelds had provided her with a warm and loving family. She never considered herself anything other than a Nietfeld.

At the Cathedral she was known for her quick wit and friendly, outgoing manner. In response to the friendly teasing of the priests, she would often come back with a snappy but appropriate comment. Her twinkling blue eyes and impish grin were her hallmark. One of the priests who had been with her at the Chancery asked her why she hadn't spoken to them in this manner there. She replied simply, "Then I was supposed to keep silence."

Helena was small in stature, like the "little people" of Irish lore. Sister Julie Ziebert, who had to stretch to reach five feet, loved to work with Helena because, she said, "Finally, I am taller than someone else." Julie's parakeet, Joy, responded to Helena's gentle personality. Invariably, when the bird was allowed freedom from the cage during community recreation, she would attack Helena's shoe laces and keep at it until they were untied. One can imagine Helena's feigned aggravation at the temerity of the little bird.

Finally, at age 82 she asked her superiors if she could retire. She had spent so many years sewing. Her eyesight was fading, but her personality was still sweet, agreeable and docile. She took up residence at Salem Heights in 1983.

Her last two years of life were spent in Emma Hall. On the evening of May 6, 1991, Helena was taken to the emergency room of Good Samaritan Hospital in Dayton. There, she died unexpectedly. To everyone's surprise, she simply slipped away.

After her death, a pamphlet entitled "The Apostolate of Smiling" was found among her belongings. One section reads, "Smile to yourself until you have warmed your own heart with the sunshine of your cheery countenance. Then go out and radiate your smiles. That smile has work to do— work to do for God." The last section of the pamphlet reads "Smile, too, at God in loving acceptance of whatever God sends into your life, and you will merit to have the radiantly smiling face of Christ gaze on you with special love throughout eternity." Those who lived and worked with Helena remember her as a happy, witty, outgoing person, and they always recalled her smile.

Hoping to find a home, the frightened little child on the orphan train who had smiled tentatively at the tall man and his wife, came at last to her real and eternal home.

Epilogue

The old sewing machines are silent. The sisters no longer require someone to make their habits. Margaret Gast, Jovita Thalheimer and Helena Nietfeld's work, though humble and unseen, fulfilled an important responsibility at the time and had great value. Because they were working for the honor and glory of God, they performed each task with exquisite love and care. Though their lives may not seem to have had a major impact on the world in which they lived, their example of fidelity to prayer and their humble service to others greatly influenced the sisters and others for whom they labored.

The value of years of quiet, humble work cannot be measured. We can only be grateful for their stories and for their example of faithfulness and great love.

Crimsoned Sands

by

Eleanor McNally CPPS

The Story of
CPPS Foundations in Arizona
(1903-1970)

Camelback Mountain silently hovers over St. Francis Cemetery in Phoenix where 14 Sisters of the Precious Blood are buried.

Prologue

Silhouetted against Arizona's brilliant blue sky is Camelback Mountain. Phoenix wouldn't be Phoenix without Camelback. She was there when all was just sun, sand, and Saguaro. She was there when the Indians graced her with their lives and culture. She was there when the pioneers came in their covered wagons and settled on the banks of the Salt River. She watched the city grow, until today Phoenix is the sixth-largest in the nation. She will be there when, at some distant time, Phoenix lies in ruins. She knows that one day she too will be gone. Camelback also knows that only in the cemetery does Eternity meet the ravages of Time and conquer. And so, in a special way, she watches over St. Francis Cemetery in the Valley of the Sun.

We wander through this quiet, sacred place until we come to the section where 14 Sisters of the Precious Blood lie. Before us is a headstone on which their names are inscribed. Read them prayerfully; read them reverently:

Sister M. Lioba Rosenhahn	1876-1904
Sister M. Petronilla Uhlmann	1896-1916
Sister M. Chrysostima Ide	1889-1918
Sister M. Apollonia Spegele	1877-1924
Sister M. Rosella Ehrbar	1860-1925
Sister M. Paschal Aspa	1902-1926
Sister M. De Sales Keane	1905-1928
Sister M. Avita Lopez	1905-1929
Sister M. Alma Magnus	1870-1930
Sister M. Dolorosa Mutter	1869-1937
Sister M. Electa Fleck	1865-1942
Sister M. Laurina Fluegel	1888-1943
Sister M. Dafrosa Huber	1872-1944
Sister M. Arimathea Greff	1907-1997

Read them gratefully for they are the pioneers of the countless women who have crimsoned the desert sands of Arizona with the Precious Blood of Jesus Christ!

In the Beginning

In the third year of the twentieth century, the Territory of Arizona had yet to be declared a state. Although the Franciscans had for years converted and baptized Indians in or near what is now Phoenix, the little adobe church of St. Mary's Parish was not founded until 1881. Within a short time, the zealous first pastor, Father Francis Jouvenceau, entreated the Sisters of Mercy to come to this sand-blown frontier town to staff two parish schools: St. Anthony's for the Spanish-speaking, and St. Mary's for the English-speaking.

The pastor's urgent requests were answered in August of 1892 when Mother Paul and four sisters arrived. They took possession of the two-story brick building built for them on unpaved, dusty Monroe Street. Here they opened a boarding and day school, which they named the Academy of the Sacred Heart. In addition, they staffed two parish schools, one on either side of the church. Attendance at all three schools increased rapidly, and more teachers came from their Motherhouse in Tucson, Arizona. In 1899 the Mercy sisters built a new convent with boarding and day school at Fourth and Monroe, the older building being retained for additional classrooms.

During this period Father Novatus Benzing OFM became pastor. Attentive to the needs of the sick and suffering, as well as to those of the school children, he importuned Mother Paul for a few more sisters to open a hospital. Torn between caring for the sick on one hand and overtaxing the sisters on the other, Mother Paul reluctantly gave in to his request. In a small six-room house on Polk Street, the sisters opened a temporary hospital which they named St. Joseph's. It was not long, however, before Mother Paul's initial fears collided on the rocks of Father Novatus's zeal.

When the priest insisted that teachers leave the lower classes of the Academy to come to the parish schools, the sisters wrote to the Bishop of Tucson, Henry Regis Granjon, asking him to release them of all teaching duties. They wished to give full time to the hospital, the first part of which was then being built on Fourth Street. In their letter, the sisters insinuated that the Franciscans were unappreciative of their efforts and wanted them out of the school.

The sisters also maintained that they were not receiving full compensation for the improvements they had made in the schools. Mother Paul upset Father Novatus further by suggesting that the parish buy the Academy so the sisters could continue building the hospital. He was adamant that any extra money in the parish be used for a new sanctuary.

Tensions became so high on both sides that the Franciscan provincial ordered the pastor to speak to the sisters only when necessary and never about money. Finally an appeal was made to Bishop Granjon who, beyond insisting that the Mexican school be kept, refused to be drawn into the argument. With no reconciliation in sight, the search began for another congregation to staff the schools.

Enter CPPS

In the winter of 1903, central Ohio lay covered with a heavy blanket of snow. Mother Emma Nunlist, Mother Superior of the Sisters of the Precious Blood, took a few hours from her busy schedule to step outdoors to meditate on the beauty of God's creation clothed in wintry white. She recalled her trip to the West a few years previously—a West with which she had fallen in love. Perhaps the snow-covered San Bernardino Mountains of Southern California reminded her of her native Switzerland. There, in 1866 at age 9, she had said *aufwiedersehen* to her homeland before coming to America with her father.

Mother Emma's vision and foresight brought Precious Blood sisters to Arizona in 1903.

After his death she was placed under the care of the Sisters of the Precious Blood and was received into the Congregation as a postulant in 1869. Deep in her heart also was the recollection of the neglected Indians and Mexicans she had met in their squalid surroundings.

Just what was Mother Emma doing in the West in the year 1896? For the answer to that question, one must look at the history of the Society of the Precious Blood, the male counterpart of the Sisters of the Precious Blood.

In 1890 the Society had sent Father Florian Hahn, the talented and "totally-converted-to-the-Indian-cause" missionary, to Banning, California. He was to open a government-supported Indian school, the stated purpose of which was to "civilize" the Indians. In spite of the prevailing attitude of the day, the priest truly loved the Indians and they loved him. He prepared some of them to be Catholic leaders; others he trained in mechanical and agricultural skills.

Florian persuaded the Sisters of St. Joseph of Carondolet to come to Banning to administer St. Boniface Grade School. Unable, however, to recruit other CPPS priests to join him in creating a community house there, Florian would later leave the Society with its blessing. He became a legend in the area, covering distances by horse and wagon even to the Mexican border. He established many missions and immersed himself completely in Indian culture. Highly respected in the Archdiocese of Los Angeles, his memory is perpetuated in the name of the church—Precious Blood—in Banning where he served.

It was at this mission in Banning that Mother Ludovica Scharf and Sister Emma stayed for the year 1896. Why were they there? The burdens of office were causing considerable stress to Mother Ludovica. In the midst of this, her throat and bronchial tubes were giving her trouble, and she was in danger of developing tuberculosis. Her doctor suggested that she spend some months in California. Taking his advice, she chose as her companion, Sister Emma, who was afflicted with a large goiter. *Not with Silver or Gold*, the Congregational history, relates the following about their memorable stay:

Father Florian and the Sisters of St. Joseph gave the two visitors a royal welcome and made their twelve-month stay at the Indian mission most pleasant and beneficial. Healthful diversions were afforded them by the lively pranks of the Indian and Mexican children, by long tramps, and by drives in a 'top-buggy' to the Indian reservations, where they observed first-hand the mode of life of the various tribes and made friends with the chiefs and their squaws.

Mother Ludovica took back with her to Ohio a souvenir of her trip that was not so pleasant—a deformity which was the result of an accident and which she was destined to carry to her grave. Several ribs having been broken in an accident caused by a runaway horse, she was never again able to sit or stand erect, but leaned far to the right from the waist. Her throat condition was improved, and she was able to resume the duties of her office.

An Invitation

Shaking the fresh snow from her cape, Mother Emma returned to the house recalling fondly her memories of the West. Going through the day's mail, she was surprised to discover a letter from a Franciscan in Arizona. Having already been refused by 16 congregations of sisters, he was begging for sisters to teach in St. Mary's School for American children and in St. Anthony's for Mexican children. Some days later, Mother Emma, who knew a sign from God when she saw it, responded:

Ehre sei dem Blute Jesu!
Maria Stein, Mercer Co, O, Dec. 31st 1902

Rev. Novatus Benzing, O.F.M.
Reverend Father:

. . . Kindly excuse the delay in replying to same. Your letter was forwarded to me, but considering the matter in question of some importance, as we have been looking for some time for an opportunity for such a field of labor for our teaching sisters in delicate health, in a mild western climate, I wanted to confer with my council before replying. Although I cannot give you any positive assurance of providing sisters for your schools at least for the present, yet I shall endeavor to promote the idea, since I am very much in favor of it.

Now, Rev. Father, I would be very thankful for some information regarding the means of subsistence. To what extent would the schools provide for a support? or, are the funds to be raised some other way? What amount of work is expected or is to be realized from the teaching sisters? Are the buildings parish property? and will you expect the sisters to open the Academy later on? You will greatly oblige me by giving me information in detail about these different points.

May God bless your efforts in his service and show us the right way to serve him also. Asking your blessing and a charitable remembrance at the holy sacrifice, I am

Yours very respectfully,
Mother M. Emma, C.PP.S.

Mother Emma wrote again on February 19 informing Father Novatus that, with the permission of Archbishop William H. Elder of Cincinnati, the Sisters of the Precious Blood would accept his offer. The recommendation of the Archbishop is worth remembering. "Your holy Sisters," he wrote, "are preparing to do in the West what the holy Magi did in the East; taking long journeys and laboring hard and suffering—all to make our Infant Savior better known and more ardently loved by many souls for whose sake He came down to earth."

First Trip to Phoenix

Wisely, Mother Emma told Father Novatus that she would like to come to Phoenix in May to see the situation for herself and to talk matters over before giving a final promise. Sister Adelaide Waltz has given us an account of Mother Emma's first trip to Phoenix:

> We still recall, how on April 20, 1903, Mother Emma with eyes sparkling with the fervor of a Saint Paul, set out upon the long and tedious journey to answer the call of the Missionaries and their flocks. Sister Victoria Drees accompanied Mother. In the hope that the balmy atmosphere and dry desert air might benefit their frail health, Sister Philothea Dick and Sister Lioba Rosenhahn, both inclined to tuberculosis, also made the journey.
>
> Settling in Arizona was considered practical also from this standpoint of health. It was hoped that the sisters who were inclined to lung trouble could recuperate while there on this mission. In many cases, when those of delicate constitutions reached these parts of the country in time, they survived and enjoyed many years of usefulness in later life while working zealously for God's little ones.

Although health reasons played a part in the decision to go to the dry lands of the Territory of Arizona, it was primarily Mother Emma's big heart that impelled her to make the fruits of the Precious Blood available in missionary lands. Supporting this was her desire to establish perpetual adoration of the Blessed Sacrament west of the Rockies. And so, with her three traveling companions, she began the long trip west. On April 25, 1903, the four sisters, after a six-day train trip, arrived in Phoenix, "a little Mexican town, a mere squatter settlement in the heart of the great desert."

Valley of the Sun

April in the Valley of the Sun is a month cozily set between the crisp air of January and the insufferable heat of July. The fragrance of orange blossoms and the song of the cactus wrens fill the air. "On all sides the giant Rockies stretch out their sinewy arms forming, as it were, a huge bowl of sunshine."

Sister Catherine of the Sisters of Mercy had been looking forward to this day when the Sisters of the Precious Blood would take over the schools. She could then be free to continue building the hospital. Warmly, she greeted Mother Emma and Sisters Victoria, Lioba, and Philothea as they stepped from the train. The sisters climbed into the wagon which, bouncing along over unpaved dusty streets, brought them to St. Mary's.

Filled with gratitude for a safe trip and with a great desire to thank their Eucharistic Lord, Mother Emma and her companions made their first stop at the Church of St. Mary's. Seeing them enter the church and observing their devout genuflection, Father Novatus nudged Brother Fritz who was with him and said, "Fritz, *nimm, dir ein beispiel!*" (Fritz, take an example!)

After the Franciscans had welcomed them enthusiastically, the four sisters were taken to their temporary lodgings in the partly-built hospital. They stayed there for eight days "attended to in all respects," until three rooms could be prepared in the school building for the sisters. Mother Emma very quickly noted the need for a convent of their own, and she put this matter into the hands of St. Joseph.

The sisters lived in the school until the end of September. Here, according to archival materials:

> The sisters roughed it in true western fashion, becoming acquainted with the natives, a mixture of Mexicans and Americans, and with the winged and crawling inhabitants of this section: the bats, horned toads, harmless lizards, woolly-legged tarantulas, unfriendly scorpions, varicolored centipedes, and scores of fat, agile, friendly cockroaches and ants.

Meanwhile St. Joseph was working. The Sisters of Mercy were eager to rid themselves of their Academy at Fourth and Monroe, and so, for $7500 it became the property of the Sisters of the Precious Blood. The sisters now had their own convent, as well as room for children who lived beyond the town and in the surrounding desert areas. The convent, which they dedicated to Our Lady of Guadalupe, had ample room for 12 to 15 sisters, plus 20 boarders. To the joy of the sisters, within two years one room was made into a chapel where "the Divine Guest could be tabernacled under the same roof."

The Pioneer Community

By September, 1903 a community of five sisters settled in the Arizona convent. Only Lioba from Tipton, Missouri remained of the group that had accompanied Mother Emma in the spring. She had come along to "recuperate from the dreadful disease of consumption." Little did she know then that on April 9, 1904 God would call her home. She would be the first sister to be buried in Phoenix "at the foot of Camelback Mountain, about six miles from the city."

The superior of these fledgling missionaries was 44-year-old Sister Hildebertha Stall, a native of Bloomville, Ohio. She arrived in early September with Sister Teresa Didier, only 22 years old, who was from Russia, Ohio. Sisters Justina Rapp and Annetta Schneider, both from Germany, came in May. Justina, just 27 years old, was to be the music teacher. Ten years later, Annetta would help found Little Flower Academy in San Luis Rey, California.

Annetta, who had a strong interest in child psychology, took over all eight grades of the Mexican school until November when she was relieved of the primary grades. In later years she would say:

> I've never believed in spanking a child to make him [sic] mind. You can do wonders with any child if God has given you the gift of being able to handle him [sic] without resorting to physical punishment. Show that child the meaning of love and you'll get the response that's needed.

No doubt these pioneers were amazed at the unbelievably high temperatures of that first summer. Nothing but wet sheets and hand fans gave them relief when the thermometer reached 115 degrees! Layer upon layer of black serge, with not even an inkling of white, served to remind them that there is probably only a screen door between Phoenix and hell.

During recreation that first year, *buenos dias* and other Spanish expressions could be heard as sisters struggled to learn the language. Some of them would be teaching Mexican children who knew little or no English! Mercer County, Ohio had not prepared them for this task! Soon they were sharing information about the Indians—Apache, Papago, Pima, Yaqui, and Navajos—whose ways and customs were so different from their experiences in the Midwest. They would also be serving other children whose families had come from all parts of the United States seeking cures for arthritis, rheumatism, asthma and consumption in this dry climate.

The seven pioneer sisters pose with one of the boarders and a statue of St. Francis Xavier, patron of missionaries.

But not all their conversation and activities were serious. Fun-loving Teresa would forget her homesickness by tucking up her habit and playing ball with Brother Fritz every day.

The sisters delighted in the fact that "the Guter Bruder Fritz spoke German and his laughter was extremely contagious." They were glad that "Brother Sixtus knew how to cook 'Suppe a la Germany'." And most of all, they appreciated that "Father Novatus towered like a sheltering oak over the small group."

The sisters quickly "learned the value of 'two bits' and that Kartoffelln and 'spuds' are one and the same." They also discovered "that praying with extended arms at any time during services, as well as throwing kisses in wild profusion to the images of the Saints, is sound, orthodox and demonstrative Catholicity in sun-broiled Arizona."

They talked about their boarders—boys and girls from all over the nation—who suffered from asthma, rheumatic fever and other non-contagious diseases. At great sacrifice, the sisters provided food and lodging for orphans, pupils from remote areas, and children from families in desperate need. These heroic women, strangers in a strange land, struggled to make Arizona a home for themselves and for the children they served. They tried to forget the thousands of miles that separated them from their Motherhouse in Maria Stein, Ohio and their loved ones. They were Precious Blood missionaries living out Christ's sacrificial offering of his blood, letting its healing power flow over the pioneer town and its desert environs!

Help Arrives

In November of 1903, additional help came from Ohio with the arrival of Sisters Zebina (Sabina) McEvoy and Valentia Braun. Valentia, a native of Wuertenberg, Germany, whose sister of the same name had died in 1899, came as cook and housekeeper. Only 31 years old when she arrived in Arizona, she is remembered as a "gentle gay soul" whose life was marked by service and suffering for others.

As for Sabina, one wonders what a McEvoy was doing among all those German names. She had come from Berlin, now Fort Loramie, Ohio, and was 34 years old. She relieved Annetta by taking over the first three grades in the Mexican school. Her Irish humor no doubt helped her deal with the cultural and linguistic mix. A good example of her free spirit is provided in a postcard written in 1939 from Rome City to a Miss Mary Binder, "Dear Mary, Kind greetings to you. Do you still have trouble in avoiding a job? I am altogether out of a job. I'm having the time of my life. In loving remembrance, Sr. M. Sabina."

Two other sisters who joined the missionaries in 1904 were Sisters Dafrosa Huber, age 31, from Botkins, Ohio and Rosella Ehrbar, age 52, from Cleveland. The latter, who had been sent west because of her weak lungs, taught in Phoenix for 12 years, "until the Lord relieved her in order to give her reward for faithful service." She died of consumption in 1925 and is buried in the Phoenix cemetery. Dafrosa, who served by doing domestic work, remained at St. Mary's for 40 years. In 1944 she died of consumption at Nazareth Sanitarium in Albuquerque, New Mexico and also awaits the final resurrection in the Phoenix cemetery.

Between 1904 and the early 1970s, approximately 300 Sisters of the Precious Blood labored in the Valley of the Sun. Among the pioneers, a number of heroic women emerge who are the stuff of legends both in the Congregation and in Arizona. Three of these sisters whose lives encompass this period, and who greatly influenced the history of the times are Sisters Esperanza Poll, Celesta Grimmelsman and Electa Fleck. Their stories form the framework of what follows.

Sister Mary Esperanza

On August 15, 1900, Euphemia Adelheid Poll received the habit of the Sisters of the Precious Blood at the Motherhouse in Maria Stein, Ohio. At the same time, as was the custom in those days, she also received a new name, "Esperanza." Was God smiling as the very German superiors gave this very German girl a very Spanish name? How long was it before the young novice realized that her name, translated into English, means HOPE? It possibly came to light on a September day in 1904. In her own words many years later, Esperanza gave an account of the exciting days that introduced her to the place where she would spend the greater part of her life—the town of Phoenix in the Territory of Arizona:

Fifty years ago, September, 1904, three of us Sisters left Ohio with Mother Emma on our way to Phoenix. Trains were not on schedule, and it took six days before we reached our destination. The Sisters had been at the station several times, but when we finally arrived, there was no one to meet us. It was a dark night, but we set out to find our way to the Convent. Here and there a dim light from an old lamp post marked out the dusty road. There was no steeple yet on St. Mary's Church to guide us, and we trudged carrying our heavy suitcases. Finally the red from the sanctuary lamp in the Convent Chapel beckoned us, and Mother Emma exclaimed, 'Oh, there is our Convent.'

We mounted the wooden steps leading to the entrance, but, alas, in the dark we could not find the doorbell. Always resigned to the will of God, Mother said, 'Let us sit on the steps and wait for the morning.' After a time I tried again to find the doorbell; this time with better luck. I rang loud and long and roused the Sisters from their slumber. In the twinkling of an eye the seven of them were at the door to give us a hearty welcome. We shook off the dust from the journey and took a short rest. When we gathered a few hours later before the tabernacle in our tiny chapel, we felt right at home in our dear little convent in Phoenix.

So far away from Ohio, the first few weeks must have brought a few tears to Esperanza's eyes. After all, it had been only

Two sisters demonstrate a Saguaro at its full height.

five years since she had left her native Germany to come to America. She had been born of honest, God-fearing, hard-working parents on November 24, 1878 in Einsburen Kreis Lingen, Hanover. She was second youngest of the family's four boys and eight girls. Four of her sisters became nuns, and one brother, a priest. Her priest brother and two of her religious sisters went to Africa as missionaries with the Marianhill Congregation, and, for a while, she contemplated following in their footsteps. By her own admission, she reneged on that idea because she had a horror of snakes.

Euphemia's next consideration was to join the Benedictine Sisters in Osnabruck, Germany. She had just returned from making inquiries there, when she received a letter from her sister, Sister Mary Camilla, who had joined the Sisters of the Precious Blood in America. Camilla wrote that Sisters Margaret Schlachter and Lidwina Koller were coming to Germany for recruits, and if Euphemia wished to join them, she should be ready. She sought the advice of a priest who, after making a novena with her, helped her come to a decision.

45

Sister Esperanza, always a beloved teacher, poses with one of her first grade classes.

Euphemia, now 26 years old, always treasured the memory of the day of her departure for America. At 3:30 in the morning, her pastor offered Mass for her with a former teacher acting as server. Undoubtedly, her loving parents were there saying good-bye forever in this life to their child. To her dying day, she would remember her mother's last words to her, "When God calls, answer!" Euphemia was torn between sadness at leaving all that was familiar to her and enthusiasm over this exciting new venture. However, her slightly-less-than-five-foot frame marched forward and never turned back.

The eager young woman arrived at Maria Stein Convent on July 27, 1899. As a novice she spent some time in Garrett, Indiana, where her older sister, Camilla, was missioned. She must have drawn comfort from her sister's presence, a precious contact with her homeland and family. Then tragedy struck. Camilla became ill with typhoid fever and died on January 20, 1901.

When Esperanza left Ohio for Arizona in 1904, it would be many years before she would again see Maria Stein and visit her sister's grave. She renewed her vows on July 26, 1906 in the little chapel of Our Lady of Guadalupe in Phoenix, and also made her final vows there on July 2, 1911. Another great day in her life—March 4, 1924—came much later when she received her naturalization papers.

First Impressions

After Esperanza arrived in Phoenix, she received her first taste of native culture in a visit to St. John's Indian Mission. The mission was 18 miles from Phoenix which in those days, we are told, amounted to a two-day trip! Here the Franciscan priests and the St. Joseph sisters boarded and educated Indian children. Once again, we have Esperanza's words:

> . . . *we made a trip in an open wagon to St. John's Mission. The roads were very dusty, and when we came to the river bed, the horses sank knee deep into the sand, and the dust was so thick we could scarcely recognize one another.*

[Note: Most rivers in Arizona for a large part of the year are completely dry!] We received a warm welcome from saintly Father Justin and good Mother de Sales and her Sisters. It was noontime and the Indian children were taking their meal of tortillas and beans. Their table was a large piece of canvas spread on the floor. This was poverty, but the big smiles of the Indians told of love and contentment.

School Begins

Within a few days, Esperanza was ready for the first day of her 54 years of teaching little ones in Arizona. This courageous pioneer, still struggling with English and only five years away from her native Germany, faced for the first time a class of little Westerners. Again we go to her own account written fifty years later:

The next day I stood before my first class of first and second graders at St. Mary's. I soon felt at home with the happy children of the West. The enrollment increased rapidly; another schoolroom was opened, and before many years we had two crowded rooms of first graders. In the course of time, many nationalities were represented: English, French, Irish, Spanish, Italian, Yugoslavic, Russian, Chinese, Japanese, and even a little Indian girl who later became a Sister of the Precious Blood. Some of the older children came on horseback or on burros. One boy would tie his donkey to a tree, and to the amusement of children and teacher, the patient animal would recite his favorite 'hee-haw,' when asked how he liked school.

Esperanza taught four generations of Catholics. A journalist from the Phoenix newspaper observed Esperanza in her fiftieth year of teaching. She reported that

. . . an inner light seemed to transform her features as she looked at her 40 little folks in one of the first grades. And you could tell by the reflected glow of love on the children's faces that Sister was something special to them, just as she must have been to the

2,000 other first graders she's nurtured, taught, and mothered.

Esperanza's Philosophy

Esperanza always held steadfast to her philosophy that educating a child is a great thing because it lays the foundation for their future. As she put it, "With the little ones you have to do the planting and someone else the reaping." Looking back over the years, she said humbly, "I have planted many seeds, and I only hope that Almighty God will bless the work so that we will have an abundant harvest for eternity." That harvest was realized in the many walks of life that her little ones eventually assumed as priests, nuns, doctors, lawyers, housewives, laborers, nurses, and teachers.

In the early days, Esperanza sometimes had as many as 80 children in her class. She taught and loved them on sweltering days in her black serge habit when the only air-conditioning was a hot breeze off the desert. She taught and loved them when every half hour the open windows brought in the clanging of street cars which, in the 1920s, had replaced the soulful braying of donkeys. She taught and loved them as, year by year, social changes affected them. Of her beloved pupils she said, "They weren't so restless then, and they minded better. Children of today see and hear much more. And they're more independent now." She was convinced, however, that all children were good, no matter what the time or circumstance.

Esperanza adapted to change in her own tranquil way. "We have to keep up with the times," she would say. Laugh lines on her face crinkled when she told of occasions when the bell rope that summoned children to the old brick school building went out of commission. "The boys used to tell me the rope broke. I'd think to myself 'Let them have their bit of fun.' " In 1926 electric bells replaced the more primitive ones.

No one in Esperanza's class ever forgot her donkey who always had a predominant place in the classroom. Where he came from no one seems to know, but his presence surely was inspired by Esperanza's love for the missions. She had only to tell her students about her brother and two sisters serving in the jungles of Durban, Natal, South Africa, to touch their hearts and pockets, as well as those of their parents.

When one of her students dropped a coin into the donkey's knapsack, the little animal would respond by saucily nodding his head. As Sister Kathryn (Arnoldine) Webster, one of sister's first graders in 1926, tells us: "We collected aluminum foil from gum, candy, etc., and rolled it into balls which sister sold for the missions." One is sure that the donkey nodded every time a new ball was presented by this ahead-of-her-time recycler. The nod of his head was enough reward to keep the pennies, nickels, and dimes coming. Even more rewarding was the fact that seeds of compassion for the less fortunate were being sown in the hearts of the children.

Esperanza received no advanced degrees. She began her high school education at Maria Stein and continued it at the Phoenix extension of the Normal School of the Precious Blood. Though she apparently had only an Arizona State Certificate, she spent every summer diligently preparing for the coming year.

Always seeking innovative ways to make learning interesting to her little ones, she had an aptitude for reaching not only the minds, but also the hearts of children. She was never fazed by the number of children in her classes. Over one five-year period, she had at least 50 boys in her first grade class. Usually, however, she had boys and girls together. Never was she more delighted than when a "colored" child entered her classroom. She looked upon each one of the 2000 plus children she taught as a beloved child of God.

Sister Esperanza taught primary grades in Phoenix for 54 years.

Beloved Community Member

Esperanza is remembered as a kind and thoughtful community member. If the sisters were told to eat three prunes in the morning just because Esperanza did, it surely was not at her orders! Faithful to the Rule, she was always a good example. She delighted new members of the Arizona community with a song she composed. Sister Rosalie Kastner recalled the words:

> O, bright and sunny Phoenix,
> You are our hearts' delight.
> From May until September
> Your sunbeams are so bright!
> It's Phoenix, It's Phoenix, the wild and woolly West!
> It's Phoenix, It's Phoenix, the wild and woolly West!

There was a second verse about Arizona's notorious sand storms, but it seems to have slipped the memories of the many sisters who once sang the song. Rosalie recalls Esperanza's kindness to her, a 17-year-old sent to teach first grade. "I didn't have any methods classes, so I relied on Sister Esperanza and copied what she had on the board and taught it the next day to my 50 children of 10 nationalities." She was not only a mentor "but an inspiration to work for the missions!" Perhaps because of her brother and sisters' ministry in Africa, Esperanza especially loved children of color and wanted them in her class."

Esperanza was known as a woman of strong principles. During the 1930s and 1940s, St. Mary's Parish sponsored an adult drama group, and the sisters often attended their performances. At one play attended by the sisters, all went well until a young lady appeared on the stage in a red evening gown cut low in the back. Shocked, Esperanza stood up, walked out, and all the nuns followed her.

If Esperanza had a fault as she grew older, it was expecting special attention because of what she termed her "advanced" age. Ultimately, Esperanza, as the oldest sister in the Phoenix convent and a real pioneer, felt that she deserved special treatment. The humble and obedient young sisters of that day usually responded to her expectations. Sister Mary Linus Bax recalls that in visiting her years later at Lourdes Hall, then the sisters' retirement home, Esperanza realized how well off she had been in Phoenix. Compared with many sisters in retirement who had far more needs than she, she decided that she had not been "truly old" when she was in Phoenix.

St. Mary's Parish celebrated Esperanza's 50 years in Phoenix on Sunday, December 12, 1954, feast of Our Lady of Guadalupe, patroness of the sisters' Chapel. She was recognized by such dignitaries as Daniel Gercke, Bishop of Tucson; Frank Murphy, Mayor of Phoenix; Howard Pyle, Governor of Arizona; and David Temple OFM, Franciscan Provincial. In the Mass of Thanksgiving on that day, Father Victor Bucher OFM referred to Esperanza as "the voice of one crying in the wilderness." The "wilderness" was the barren Arizona desert to which the young German nun had come in 1904.

Somewhat overwhelmed by the Jubilee celebration, she said humbly, "I have done only what every other sister does—stayed where they put me." Then, with a little chuckle, she added, "But I was glad to stay!" Sister climaxed the Jubilee program with her first public speech, delivered like a veteran, to an audience of more than 400 admirers. She was at her best as she left to her former pupils her great lesson: "We must all meet in Eternity!"

Statehood for Arizona

The bestowing of statehood on Arizona must have been an exciting day for Esperanza, the faculty, and the students at St. Mary's as we read in the following from a contemporary document:

> In 1912 Arizona became the 48th state of the Union. Admission Day, February 14, was a gala day for entire Arizona and particularly for Phoenix. All the school children of the city paraded the streets and listened to patriotic speeches. The pupils of St. Mary's School were dressed in red, white, and blue sashes for the occasion. The boys were placed in the charge of the Franciscan Fathers, while several ladies of the parish volunteered to chaperone the girls.

The Sisters were anxious that their pupils carry off the honors of the day for good behavior. Some of the Sisters decided to walk to the corner of Fourth and Washington Streets and there, safely hidden in the crowds of spectators, watch the children pass by. Each school was to carry some distinguishing emblem. St. Mary's delegation carried a home-made banner of blue velvet bearing the words ST MARY'S SCHOOL inscribed in large gilt letters.

Washington Street was not paved at this time, and the steady tramp of the marchers churned the loose sand so that stifling clouds of dust descended on the spectators, blinding and choking them and, at times, completely hiding from view children and banners. 'Twas a festive day for Phoenix and one never-to-be-forgotten by loyal Arizonians, young and old!'

Arizona was known as the "Baby State" until the addition of Hawaii and Alaska took away that nickname. With statehood came improved water and lighting facilities, paved streets, and a general air of progress. The sleepy little town of 12,000 in 1903 was waking up and smelling the desert flowers!

St. Mary 's Grammar School

The formal name of the school where Esperanza was a teacher during her early days in Phoenix was St. Mary's Grammar School. At first she taught in the red brick building designated for English-speaking children on the Fourth Street side of the Church. St. Mary's and St. Anthony's were the only Catholic schools in that part of the Territory of Arizona. Both schools enjoyed a fine reputation for the ability of their teachers.

An unsigned document advertising the school gives some idea of the quality of the education provided at St. Mary's:

The education was of a most practical character, the course of study pursued through the primary and grammar school grades being almost identical with that followed in the public schools. Every attention is given to the moral and religious training of the pupils, and their general deportment is equally of unremitting care.

Vocal and instrumental music—piano, guitar, mandolin and violin, are taught according to the most approved methods, while plain and ornamental sewing, a great auxiliary to the cultivation of taste, is also a specialty in the school. In this age of infidelity and indifference in religion a Catholic education is a necessity. Catholic parents are obliged to send their children to Catholic schools in order that the child, through example and precept, may be brought up a practical Catholic. It is our duty then to encourage, both by word and work, this worthy undertaking so much calculated to bring souls to God.

St. Mary's Parish Church, built in 1914, was designated as a basilica in 1985 and is a national historical monument.

The above account was followed by this announcement:

> The convent opens in the latter part of September and closes in June. Accommodations have been made for a limited number of boarders. Rates may be had on application to Sister Superior Mary Electa at the school. Several medals and other prizes are awarded to the successful pupils in general excellency, Christian doctrine, needle work and other subjects at the end of each term.

By 1926 Immaculate Heart, a new parish for Mexicans, built a school a few blocks from St. Mary's and brought Immaculate Heart sisters from Mexico to staff it. Since Spanish-speaking students began attending the new school, this marked the end of St. Anthony's. Precious Blood sisters for a time concentrated their efforts on St. Mary's which by this time also included a high school.

Schools Added

In 1958 education was further advanced in the Valley of the Sun when the pastor of Sacred Heart Parish in southeast Phoenix, Father Albert Brown, in true Franciscan pioneering spirit built a school. Since Precious Blood sisters had been going to Sacred Heart weekly for religion classes for many years, it was taken for granted that they would teach the Mexican children in the new school. Sister LaSalette Hageman was the first principal.

Not far from St. Mary's another mission church, St. Mark's, opened a four-room school in 1959, staffed by the Sisters of the Precious Blood who had done catechetical ministry there for some years. Sister Elise Calmus recalls that, besides being principal, she taught seventh and eighth grades. In her first graduating class was a young man who, 38 years later, became her boss in the administration department of the University of Arizona! Years later, the Sisters of the Precious Blood served at Gerard and Bourgade High Schools and at St. Thomas the Apostle Parish School in Phoenix.

55

The beautiful new St. Mary's School, built in 1926 on the corner of Fourth and Van Buren, cost $250,000. St. Anthony's School was replaced by the new monastery, and the site of old St. Mary's became playground space. The new school flourished, and during the 1940s and 1950s, boasted an enrollment of 650 students with 15 teaching sisters.

Times changed, however, and as Phoenix grew, families moved from the metropolitan area into the suburbs. By 1978 there were only five teaching sisters at St. Mary's, and by 1983 only one sister, Sister Nancy Wolf, remained as principal. Enrollment declined until only a little over 100 were in attendance. The school closed in 1994 with great sadness on the part of the Franciscans, the Sisters of the Precious Blood, many lay teachers, and thousands upon thousands of alumni.

Esperanza's Last Days

Buildings and people age. So too did Esperanza. She suffered from a chronic heart condition, and in 1958, retirement at Salem Heights seemed her best option. Esther Clark of the Phoenix *Gazette* wrote, "Some of the Arizona sunshine will go with Sister Mary Esperanza when she leaves Phoenix tonight after 54 years of teaching."

And how did Esperanza feel about leaving Arizona? In her simple, conformity-to-God's-will style, she said, "I'm going to miss Arizona and its friendly people." As she boarded the TWA Super Constellation for her very first plane ride, did she think of the six-day train ride 54 years earlier and that long trudge through the night to the darkened convent? Perhaps! But surely, as the plane circled over South and Camelback Mountains, she looked down on all the little seeds she had planted in the Valley of the Sun and, as was her wont, sprinkled prayers on the little ones she had loved so much.

Esperanza spent 13 years at Salem Heights. Occasionally she was asked, "How could you leave Phoenix?" She would respond with her deep spirit of faith, "I think I would be foolish if I would say that I couldn't leave Phoenix, after I had left my own home and fatherland to come to America to serve

God." Her reply reflected the deep impression made on her by her mother's words, "When God calls, answer."

Esperanza spent much time before the Blessed Sacrament praying for missionaries and sinners. In spite of failing vision, she made bandages to be used for lepers because she never forgot her siblings in Africa. On December 8, 1970, a few weeks before her death, 92-year old Esperanza wrote the following to Sister Anaclete Kirwan, then stationed in Phoenix:

> *Many thanks to you, dear Sister, for your many kindnesses. I enjoyed every card, letter, etc., you sent me. I know, you will forgive me—as my fingers often jump the line and my memory likes to slip. Sometimes it works better than other times. But the Little Babe of Bethlehem will repay all.*
>
> *I am so glad you love your work in the West, and I know you enjoyed the grand celebration of St. Mary's and the city of Phoenix. For so many years St. Mary's was the only Catholic church in the vast region, and I'm sure the angels counted the many footprints of the good Franciscan Fathers (and sweat drops too) as they were walking through the hot sand and sparkling sunshine to distant sick calls to a poor Mexican or Indian. The St. Joseph and Franciscan Sisters did their work in the desert too, and still do.*
>
> *Well, dear Sister, what does it matter where we are working or what we do? Just so the Master finds us ready, when at life's evening, He calls us home. What joy, when we all shall meet in our heavenly home! . . .There are so many stray sheep. Let us ask the dear Infant at Xmas to bring them home. . . .*
>
> *Now, dear Sister, I'll place my good wishes for you and all of your Sisters in the Sacred Heart of our Little King when He comes to our hearts in the Holy Night. God bless you. Greetings from our Sisters in Emma Hall.*
>
> *Love and greetings,*
> *Sr. M. Esperanza*

On January 31, 1971, having fulfilled all the HOPE of her Spanish name, Esperanza took the hand of her loving Master, and together they walked from the thirsty desert of this world to the green pastures of Paradise.

Sister Mary Celesta

It takes all kinds to bring about the reign of God! If Sister Esperanza was the ideal first grade teacher, then Sister Mary Celesta Grimmelsman emerged as the slender aristocratic administrator. If Esperanza was the HOPE of the early Precious Blood community, then Celesta represented their FAITH. Esperanza's influence helped to bring the humble beginnings of the Sisters of the Precious Blood in Phoenix to full maturity. Celesta, in 1917, created the first Catholic secondary school in the state—St. Mary's High School—with nothing but two borrowed classrooms, four typewriters, and 17 students.

Alice Grimmelsman, the daughter of George and Frances (Ronnebaum), was born in Cincinnati, Ohio on October 8, 1886. She was one of six children, five of whom in adulthood served the Church directly. Two sisters, Sister Teresa Frances and Sister Cecile, joined the Sisters of Charity in Cincinnati; two brothers became diocesan priests, with one of them, Henry, eventually becoming a Bishop.

Alice spent her high school years at Cedar Grove Academy in Cincinnati. Little is known of her early life except that she was always a quiet, reserved person. How she became acquainted with the Sisters of the Precious Blood, and why she chose this farm community in Mercer County, Ohio over the Charities of metropolitan Cincinnati can only be speculated.

At the age of 23, she entered the Sisters of the Precious Blood at Maria Stein Convent on March 15, 1910. She professed her first vows on August 15, 1913 and her final vows on the same day in 1920. After teaching for five years at various missions in Ohio, she was sent to Catholic University in Washington D.C. where, in 1917, she received her A.B. degree with a major in English and minors in history, Latin, and German.

Arizona Bound

Armed with the sophistication of a degree and the propriety of the Midwest, Celesta and her companion, Sister

Mary Pancratia Berting, headed by train to the untamed West with the assignment to open a high school in Phoenix. Always a very private person, Celesta gave no evidence of the volleys of doubt that swirled around in her mind as she watched the fruited plains of the Midwest become the prairies of Nebraska and Kansas, then the Rocky Mountains, and finally the great Sonoran Desert!

By the time Celesta and Pancratia arrived in Phoenix, the grammar school had been operating successfully for 14 years. Upon graduation from the elementary school, however, students had no option except to attend the local public high school, Phoenix Union. Father Novatus had appealed to Mother Emma to send sisters to open a secondary school. Eager to continue the fine academic education and moral development the students were receiving at St. Mary's, the Sisters of the Precious Blood said "Yes." In doing so, they agreed to attempt an almost impossible task. They would found the first Catholic high school in the state of Arizona. Celesta, now 31, and Pancratia, 32, faced an enormous challenge.

Phoenix in 1917

By 1917 the city had grown to 124 miles of dusty streets, 35 miles of paved avenues, 64 miles of sidewalks, and 21 miles of streetcar lines. No grand school building, such as those in the Midwest, greeted Celesta and Pancratia on their arrival. Rather, they soon learned that two empty classrooms on the second floor of St. Anthony's School for Mexicans would be all they would have that first year. Did they go to bed that first night wondering what in the world awaited them? Did they sit down with Father Novatus the next day and plan strategy? Surely it was their faith that gave them the courage to bring to birth St. Mary's High School, tiny, but filled with the promise of the future.

Celesta and Pancratia spent the summer in preparation and, most assuredly, they made one act of faith after another. This was especially true when they discovered, upon inspecting the two rooms, only a piano, a life-size picture of the

Guardian Angel, a gas plate, a sewing machine, and a cupboard full of odd unwashed dishes and several tubs. Not a desk or a book was in sight! Too quickly, September 17, 1917, the opening day of school arrived. An anonymous historian gave us this record:

> Upstairs, standing in one of two sparsely furnished classrooms, Celesta and Pancratia exchanged smiles along with glances of confidence and joy. It was early morning, but already the sun's rays were harbingers of the day's intense heat. 'It seems like a dream that we are opening a Catholic high school here,' Celesta said as she led the way down a sturdy staircase onto a sidewalk. For a long moment the nuns gazed at the neighboring surroundings. Across the unpaved Monroe Street were private dwellings. Down the dusty street moved a leisurely melange of buggies, horses, donkeys, bicyclists, and a few slow-moving pedestrians.
>
> For the nuns, this was a dramatic day—the beginning of an educational saga, the launching of St. Mary's High School. 'It doesn't look like any of our high schools in the East, but at least it is a beginning,' declared Celesta as she turned and observed the simple exterior of the second floor of St. Anthony's. No wonder a deep feeling of joy, a first-nighter sense of anticipation, filled the air as Celesta

Sister Celesta was the first principal of St. Mary's High School.

greeted the first class of five boys and twelve girls. Like Pied Pipers, she and Pancratia led the historic first class of St. Mary's High to the second floor.

Classes Begin

Until books arrived, classes were conducted according to university methods—lectures by the two teachers. Celesta was fulltime teacher of English, mathematics, and science; Pancratia taught the commercial subjects, and a Franciscan priest was instructor of religion. Card tables sagging dangerously to one side and a motley collection of chairs sufficed until proper school desks could be obtained. A version of these early days comes from Lottie Weisel, one of the pioneer group of students:

> I can remember those early high school days quite well. There was no cooling as today and tuition was $5.00 a month, plus book expenses. We had two classrooms, and all the students sat around a single table, studying algebra, Latin and Spanish. Despite our unusual start above the elementary school, I recall that we had four typewriters available for our typing classes.
>
> From the outset of the school, rules of behavior were established. The girls wore no make-up and we had no uniforms until later. Every morning the girls had to line up for skirt length inspection. Our skirts had to hit a string the Sisters had stretched across a certain area in the classroom. And believe me they had to hit the cord at the correct level or we would hear about it!

In an interview for *The Knight*, St. Mary's High School's publication, on the occasion of her 50 years in the Congregation, Celesta was asked, "What was St. Mary's like way back then?" She answered in her typical self-effacing way:

Well, it was located on the corner of Third and Monroe where the rectory now stands. Instead of soft green grass nourished by the bright Phoenix sun, there was nothing but heavy, hot sand for miles around. Even the horny toads enjoyed visiting and did so quite frequently. In fact, it was a rather trying task to rid the school of them.

Celesta then volunteered that, of all the trials that she and Pancratia encountered, the one that brought the most inconvenience was the lack of coolers—not even a fan! If lucky, students might have the privilege of sitting at desks, she said; if not, they sat on the floor! Then, with a sparkle in her eyes and her Mona Lisa smile, she ended the interview.

Sister Mary Pancratia

Pancratia shared credit with Celesta for the founding of St. Mary's High School and its subsequent success. She was

born in Minster, Ohio on October 1, 1885 and given the name Isabella. Preceded in the Congregation by two sisters, Sister Mary Theresita and Sister Mary Auxilia, Isabella entered in 1911. The story is told that while traveling west by Pullman with Celesta, she broke her glasses. On her arrival in Phoenix, Sister Mary Electa Fleck, the superior, told her not to worry as there was a harness shop in Phoenix if she really needed a new pair!

With shock number one over, Pancratia settled down to class preparations and became a remarkable business teacher. Unfortunately, an accident caused her to lose the

Sister Pancratia and her sister, Sister Theresita, share a quiet moment in the Arizona sunshine.

use of her right hand. While scrubbing the floor, she got a splinter in her hand which became infected; as a result, the hand eventually became useless. Pancratia always wore a white mitt on that hand, but the injury did not lessen her effectiveness as a teacher.

It wasn't long before Phoenicians were heaping praise on the commercial class of the school. Well-trained and efficient graduates found important positions both in the private sector and in city, state, and other government positions. One businessman wrote to Celesta:

> Graduates from the commercial department [of St. Mary's] are competent and finished in every manner; in fact so much so, that in addition to the usual duties contemplated by the course they have had, [they] are entrusted with matters requiring executive ability which of course could be practical only because of the preliminary training available in your school.

A letter from the Sister Superior of St. Joseph's Hospital seconded the praise:

> The superiority of the commercial training given at St. Mary's Girls' High School was evidenced by all four [graduates] who took the positions in the clerical department of the Hospital. The readiness with which they adapted themselves to Medical and Nursing phraseology and the rapidity with which their efficiency was demonstrated proved the thoroughness of their preparation for the business world.

Not to be outdone by the business students, graduates from the classical courses also reaped their bit of praise. Joseph L. Schmitt, the only boy in the first graduating class, went on to a life of substantial achievement. After graduation from high school in 1921, he obtained his B.S. and Ph.D. degrees. He organized his own insurance company, Modern Pioneers Life Insurance, becoming its director, chairman of the board, and president.

Joe was remarkable for a number of "firsts." He piloted the first commercial plane into the Grand Canyon for Warner Brothers. He investigated the field of tabulation, the grandfather of computers. As a result of his education in mechanical engineering, he was responsible for installing the first mechanical accounting system in Maricopa County.

In addition to Joseph Schmitt, many doctors, nurses, lawyers, teachers and a considerable number of priests and sisters came from St. Mary's in those early days. In 1930 the Dean of Women at Phoenix Junior College wrote a highly commendatory letter to Sister Mary Celesta, who was still principal. Among other things, she wrote:

> You have every reason to be proud of your students. I think that I can say in fairness to everyone that they are above the average that come to us. I have remarked to some of the girls from St. Mary's that I thought they must have unusually good training over there.

Moral Development

Beyond the academic, St. Mary's was outstanding in the development of moral character. A Christian atmosphere was maintained, and the high ideals set forth by the Church were presented to the students at all times. A graduate of St. Mary's Class of 1923 wrote, "I am keenly aware of the value of the thorough training which St. Mary's offers its students. This training includes not only unusual efficiency along academic lines but offers as well character-building facilities." This alumnus continued concerning a St. Mary's graduate in his office, saying:

> She is only one of a number of graduates of St. Mary's High School coming within my observation whom I regard as an outstanding credit to the kind of training offered by St. Mary's. The ability with which she accomplishes her everyday tasks, the courtesy which she accords not only visitors to the office but

her superiors, and the keen sense of responsibility which she manifests, reflect with credit the teaching she has enjoyed at the hands of the Venerable Sisters comprising the faculty of St. Mary's.

Although this wonderful academic and spiritual training began in two rooms with only 17 students in 1917, Celesta and Pancratia's faith blossomed with a little help from Father Novatus and the Franciscans. In 1919 they began building a one-story stucco structure for classrooms directly across the street from St. Mary's Church.

Before the structure was completed, Sister Mary Nathalia Smith, fresh from Catholic University with her A.B. degree, joined the faculty. Since there was no more room in the Mexican school, she set up classes in the church basement where she taught courses in Spanish, American history, mathematics, general science, and chemistry. Nathalia commented that, when the new building was completed, there was great rejoicing on the part of teachers and students. They could leave their crowded and often very hot quarters for delightful new classrooms.

This was the same year that Central Arizona Gas and Light came into being, and so the new classrooms could be heated in the chilly winter months with gas stoves resembling radiators. A tunnel was built under Monroe Street from the grade school yard to the high school, and heat was piped from the furnace in the grammar school.

First Graduation

In June, 1920 the first class graduated from St. Mary's—five girls and one boy. Ceremonies took place in one of the classrooms. The outstanding feature of the day was a solemn High Mass in St. Mary's Church with many priests in the sanctuary. This was a momentous occasion—the first Catholic high school graduation in the state of Arizona!

Professional that she was, from the beginning Celesta affiliated the struggling high school with the Catholic University in Washington, D.C. In 1940 she did the same with the University of Arizona, thus making it a fully accredited high school. In the beginning, Celesta taught every course, from first year subjects to more advanced classes. In addition to her heavy teaching schedule, she was principal, and moderator of the Sodality of the Blessed Virgin, then a flourishing group.

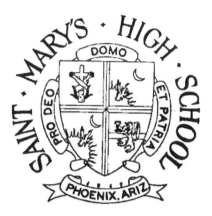

*The insignia of the Sisters of the Precious Blood (lower right)
on the shield of St. Mary's High School serves as a reminder
of the dedication of the early sisters.*

Not long after the founding of the high school, Celesta and Pancratia began their mission work at the Indian School at Kimatke. Pancratia catechized and brought to Baptism the grandson of Geronimo. She had a less fulfilling moment as she was preparing Indian boys for their four-times-a-year confession. One six-footer said to her, "If you didn't talk so much, I could find my sins!"

How did these two catechists get to the mission and back? Being open and willing to do whatever was necessary, they drove there in a Model T Ford! Celesta would crank the car while Pancratia fiddled with the spark arrester. Then Celesta, the driver, would get in and put her hands on the wheel. With four floor pedals—clutch, brake, reverse and gas—to manipulate, she would take off for their missionary work. Sister Clara Van DeBeuken, then a child, remembers well the scene of the two sedate nuns

Sisters gather in 1928 on the 25th anniversary of arrival in Arizona of the Sisters of the Precious Blood.

with black veils flying, barreling down the road at 20 miles an hour! Quiet, reserved Celesta never talked about these things. She went about doing good, never giving a thought to her uniqueness even in her later years.

Sister Mary Fidelis

In 1920 a second story was added to the high school. The following year Sister Mary Fidelis Froelich, who had been teaching in the grade school, joined the high school faculty. She provided much needed relief for Celesta by taking over Latin and English classes and the library. Fidelis was a valuable addition to the staff. Born Ida Froelich in Mud Creek (Defiance), Ohio in 1898, she entered the convent at 18 years of age. During her career, she had various teaching and librarian assignments, but she is remembered primarily for her 20 years at St. Mary's High School. Her five-by-five frame was cheerfully referred to by the boys as "FiFi," but she never let on that she was aware of it. The community publication, *Ave Regina,* provided the following description of Fidelis:

> During many of her years she was a librarian. This role gave her beautiful personality a chance to shine out clearly. She was eminently patient, kind, and helpful with the high school students who felt free at any time to ask, or even clamor, for her service. Sister had a fund of humor that could make an occasional 'Now find it yourself' a challenge and not a rejection.
>
> Sister's patience and good humor made her a pleasant companion to live with. Her sisters remember also her ever-ready willingness to give help of any kind. Sister Pancratia remembers how her own years of active service in Phoenix were lightened and brightened by Fidelis who was always ready to do the work of Sister Pancratia's crippled hand unobtrusively and without being asked.

69

By the time Fidelis arrived in 1921, Phoenix had grown to a population of 44,000, and its original city limits of 16th Street to 19th Avenue between Washington and Roosevelt were beginning to bulge. So was St. Mary's High School which was approaching five times its original number of students. St. Mary's lost Nathalia in 1924 when she returned east; Cortona from St. Anthony's replaced her. Fidelis, ever the librarian historian, recounts a bit about the school in those days:

> Each Christmas the students had a Christmas gift exchange and received some little gift such as pictures or a little crib set, from the faculty. On the Sunday or some day close to Christmas, the older members of the school would put on a Christmas play. These were plays that Sister Pancratia wrote herself for the occasion. She wrote all of the plays attempted by the students of St. Mary's during her stay there.

The last three years of Fidelis' life were spent in the library and the Mother Brunner Shrine at the Motherhouse in Dayton. Always true to her name, "Fidelis," she was ready when God called on January 7, 1972.

Brophy Preparatory College

In 1928 the Jesuits at St. Francis Parish opened Brophy Preparatory College for boys. Because nearly all the boys from St. Mary's transferred to the new school, St. Mary's enrollment dropped from 86 to 63. Undaunted, the nuns carried on. The next year disaster struck the school and the entire nation with the beginning of the Great Depression. Would bad times cause St. Mary's to lose more students?

Money was scarce, but the education of youth continued at St. Mary's. Fidelis tells us that "any student who came to register for classes was always admitted by the pastor, Father Novatus, and by Sister Celesta, regardless of whether or not he or she had funds. Many came hungry," she remembers, "but with the little we had, they were fed and educated. No child was refused entrance to St. Mary's High School."

By 1930 students were coming to St. Mary's High from all over the Valley. Many made the long trek from Flagstaff, Globe, and Superior. They came by foot, by streetcar, and by automobile, driving in from Tolleson, Tempe, and Mesa. Many students continued to board at the convent. By 1931 the enrollment has risen to 100. That same year Phoenix had its first building with refrigeration—the Fox Theater!

Brophy Preparatory College, plagued by financial problems, folded in 1936, and Father Martin Knauff OFM, now pastor at St. Mary's, contemplated building a boys' high school on "Polk Lot," which had been purchased in 1920 by a far-seeing Father Novatus. A drive for funds was initiated, and by 1938, the school with 17 classrooms was completed at a cost of $90,000. Finally, the dream of a great football team could be realized, a far cry from the stumbling efforts of the boys of early St. Mary's who, in spite of the odds, had managed to capture two trophies, one in '24 and the other in '27.

Because of the increased enrollment, graduation in 1941 of both boys and girls could no longer be held in a classroom as in the beginning, or in the church hall. For the first time it took place at Encanto Park with Bishop Daniel Gercke officiating.

Celesta's Gifts

Celesta's 23 years as teacher and principal at St. Mary's came to a close in 1942 when she returned to Dayton to become principal of Precious Blood High School at Salem Heights. The 1942 Chapter called her to be fourth councilor under Mother Mary Magna Lehman, serving at the same time as superior of the Motherhouse. Four years later, the Chapter elected Nathalia, Celesta's long-time friend from Phoenix, as Mother Superior. On the first ballot, Celesta was elected Vicaress.

Very little is recorded of Celesta's contribution in these positions. Once again her retiring ways got things going, but with an effective little piccolo rather than a mighty trumpet. Completing her term as Vicaress in 1954, Celesta was assigned as local superior to the scene of her pioneering days— Phoenix, Arizona. Already 71 years of age, Celesta also became Regional Superior of the West in 1957, while still retaining her position in St. Mary's convent until 1960.

In later years as she walked to St. Mary's Church, what were her thoughts and feelings when she glanced at the high school? Unfortunately for posterity, she never alluded to her courageous pioneer days. It was also characteristic of her that she never spoke of her talent as a gifted pianist. Sister Mary Kathryn (Palmarita) Gurren, who taught with her in the early days, recalls her accompanying the sisters when they sang.

Sisters who lived with Celesta in the fifties, remember her as a rather strict superior, but also as one who never demanded of others what she did not demand of herself. Her spirituality resembled the asceticism of a John of the Cross rather than the childlike joy of a Little Flower. Though never unkind, she often disappointed sisters who tried to add fun and variety to the recreation period. The "Philo Coterie," a group devoted to discussion of philosophy, was short-lived; the chess players were discouraged. Fidelity to the Rule, as she understood it, was paramount.

That there was a gentler side to Celesta is apparent from the fact that during recreation she permitted square dancing, a welcome outlet especially for the younger sisters. She also encouraged the "Merry Grayettes," a musical group conducted by Sister Mary (Florian) Shearman. Once a year, at a tea for parents of the sisters, this group provided entertainment. Celesta was an understanding person, always ready to listen when a sister needed to unload. With about forty sisters in the house, the good superior dried many a tear unseen by anyone but her.

Sister Mary Louise (Hilary) Barhorst recalls the warm, human side of Celesta. When Mary Louise was only 29 and a student at Immaculate Heart College in Los Angeles in 1956, she was appointed principal and superior of Queen of Peace School in Mesa, Arizona. However, the sister in charge of the summer sisters at the college, for some reason, questioned the appointment and did not give Hilary her obedience until she called Celesta. In no uncertain terms, Celesta informed the sister that the obedience was correct. "When I got home to Phoenix," Mary Louise said, "Celesta was very supportive and instructed me to give her a call whenever I had any questions. In fact, she accompanied me on the trip to Mesa. . . . I survived with the help of Celesta."

Celesta celebrated 50 years in religious life in 1960. On hand for the celebration was her brother, Bishop Henry Grimmelsman of Evansville, Indiana, whose installation as bishop she and Florian had attended in Cincinnati in 1944. At a beautiful celebration in her honor, St. Mary's Parish presented her with a burse for a young woman aspiring to become a Precious Blood sister. As Celesta cut the anniversary cake, she shared joyful memories with the many who came to the reception. One who attended remarked: "Sister has given expression of her dedicated life by sharing her mind and heart with all God's children who came to listen and to learn the way through life with God, her dominant love."

Retirement

When the time came for her to retire to Salem Heights, Celesta performed clerical tasks for as long as she was able. Eventually arterial sclerotic heart disease took its toll, and Celesta went to Lourdes Hall. The Tao tradition calls the perfection of maturity the "child with wisdom." Jesus admonished, "Unless you become as little children. . . ." Everyone arrives at this point in her own way.

For Celesta, who toward the end was secured in her chair for reasons of safety, it included her gently pleading with visitors to "please get the glue off my chair so I can get up." Or she would entertain with the story of that wonderful roll of paper with its little squares that she could keep folding. Sister Eileen (Pat) Crother, who would feed her in those final days, recalls fondly how simple and childlike she had become. Celesta, no longer under the ascetical hand of John of the

Cross, now had the freedom of a child to express whatever was on her mind.

On July 27, 1968, Celesta's life of FAITH quietly came to an end. Perhaps Esperanza took the hand of her old friend from Phoenix, and together, as children of wisdom, they entered the joys of heaven.

St. Mary 's High Continues

In the years following Celesta's departure from Arizona, other great men and women carried on the work she had begun. Sisters of the Precious Blood and Franciscan Friars continued the great tradition of the early pioneers as the school underwent many changes and permutations. It became coed once again in 1957, using both the Polk Street and Monroe Street sites. Later the Polk Street location became quite valuable in the urban renewal of Phoenix. In 1988 it was sold for $5,500,000—quite an increase over the $20,000 purchase price in 1920.

The school was moved to an educational building a few miles north which was renovated and expanded into an attractive modern school. St. Mary's High still flourishes on the corner of Third and Sheridan. It is the largest Catholic high school in Arizona with an enrollment of about 800, 60% of whom are minority students. Its superior academic programs with modern technology are a long way from the four typewriters of 1917. There is still a fierce pride in its record of first-rate football teams. Since the school still does not have its own football field, it continues to use city parks for practices as it did when it was a small poor school with feisty players struggling against the larger public schools.

In 1981 the last Precious Blood sister teaching at St. Mary's High, Sister Carol Ann Muller, left the school. Yet the memory of the sisters continues. In the new school there is a wing called Celesta Hall on which there is a mural depicting the early days of the school complete with a likeness of Celesta in a black habit. A current source reports:

St. Mary's student body still carries on the goals of that small group of pioneering students in 1917 and its teaching staff of two courageous nuns. It continues on with its family spirit of faith and love. It keeps high the words inscribed on the Knights' shield: 'For God, Home, and Country.'

Sister Celesta's face can be seen in this detail from a large mural on the outside of Celesta Hall at St. Mary's High School

Sister Mary Electa

"There remain Faith, Hope and Love, but the greatest of these is LOVE." Of all the sisters who have served in Arizona, probably no one exemplified the love of our foundress, Maria Anna Brunner, more than Sister Mary Electa Fleck. "From the very beginning," a 1937 document reports, "the Sisters in the West followed the practice of their blessed Foundress . . . and interested themselves in poor and orphan children." Electa's response to the orphans and the poor, her concern for Mexicans and Indians, and her warm, understanding relationship with the sisters was evident over and over again in her 31 years in Phoenix.

The United States was in the final month of the Civil War when, on March 16, 1865, Mary (Vehorn) and John Fleck of Maria Stein, Ohio welcomed into the world their little Mary. Judging from her adult years, Mary was a good little girl with a smile for everyone and a gift for knowing what others needed and responding without fanfare. When Mary was 14, she was happy to greet a baby sister, Margaret, who would later

The chapel in the convent at St. Mary's was built in 1925.

become Sister Mary Eusebia and would serve with Electa in Phoenix for 23 years.

At 22 years of age, Mary answered the call to religious life by entering the Maria Stein Convent, a few miles from her home. She was received as a novice in 1888. As Sister Mary Electa, she taught at Wanatah, Indiana in 1889, studied at Grunenwald, Ohio in 1890, and made her first vows in 1891. The young sister was then sent to Dayton where she served as directress of St. Joseph Orphanage until 1899. After a year of doing domestic work at Maria Stein and a year as superior at New Reigel, she was again assigned as directress of the Orphanage, a position she held for ten more years. In 1911 came the biggest surprise of all—a train ticket to Phoenix! She would spend the rest of her days in the Valley of the Sun.

Phoenix Convent Remodeled

Electa arrived in Phoenix at a time when remodeling the convent to accommodate the bulging number of sisters and boarders was going full-steam ahead. Five years prior to Electa's arrival, Mother Emma had come to Phoenix as superior. Her term of office as Mother Superior had ended and she was in poor health. After some time at St. Mary's, she initiated a much-needed renovation of the convent. An early sister historian reports the following:

> The Western gophers had made frantic attempts to be friendly with the Strangers from the East and in their enthusiasm to visit the Sisters had practically eaten their way through the delicately tinted pink front steps and the less pretentious back kitchen steps that led to the Sisters' Culinary Art Department. Hence Mother Emma found herself compelled to use drastic measures against the vigorous would-be visitors and to replace the wooden steps with cement ones.
>
> The interior of the convent also was renovated and remodeled to suit requirements. A room was set aside and fitted up for the Eucharistic Lord. With

Christ, the Master, safely housed in their midst, the sharp edge was taken away from many of the privations and hardships that the Sisters were called upon to endure. Before the building-reform program had been successfully concluded, Mother Emma was recalled to the East to take up again the heavy cross of [being] Mother General. She therefore delegated Sister Electa . . . to take her place to further the work she had begun.

With the advent of the new superior, the garden which bordered the sidewalk to the west yielded to a new west wing, while a similar wing was added to the original building on the east to secure exterior symmetry of design. Interior accommodations for the growing family of Sisters and a notable increase of boarders and poor children were woven into the building plans. The second floor of the new west wing was destined for a chapel and although the Sisters' faces, in the ensuing years, visibly streamed with the ardor of devotion, the new chapel was the ideal trysting place where Spouse met Spouse in heart-to-heart converse.

Electa as Superior

Even with these improvements, Electa discovered that there was still need for further expansion. Sisters were asking for more playground space so essential to the physical well-being of the youngsters and the sisters' peace of mind. The chicken yard and the hen house had to go. Since there was no room to the west, north or south, Electa sought the property to the east, belonging to a Mrs. Kane. But that dear lady had no intention of selling. As a last resort, a statue of St. Joseph was buried on the property "in accordance," said Electa, "with traditional Catholic faith." It took several years for St. Joseph to influence the good Mrs. Kane to sell, but eventually the property was acquired. As a result, the boys enjoyed a new dormitory; Sister Attala Missler, new music rooms; and the Sisters of the Precious Blood, a whole half block of Phoenix property!

Sister Electa, with 18 years' experience at St. Joseph's Orphanage in progressive Dayton, faced an entirely different situation in Phoenix. A chronicle of the times describes early conditions:

> Arizona had not yet been admitted to statehood, and primitive methods of labor were common to all. The Sisters were no exception, and thus the weekly washday duties were performed in the open. During the rainy season the Sisters watched for the opportune moment between showers to dash from the shelter of the basement into the yard to stir the clothes in the wash boiler and to rub a few pieces on the board.

Other memories recall that articles of clothing were stolen from the wash line and that sisters often lost their overshoes, during the rainy season, when crossing muddy Fourth Street to church and school.

Phoenix had been pure desert before the construction of the Roosevelt Dam in 1911, and then it blossomed into an oasis. The city became a network of irrigation ditches and unpaved roads. Shopping on irrigation days was a challenge. Since the foot planks provided were inadequate for the number of shoppers, the sisters, along with everyone else, had to learn how to hop dry shod over the ditches.

The convent yard itself was decorated with ditches. It was the duty of the superior to open them every fifth day for the sisters' quota of water; then, when the ditches were filled to the brim, to close them. This must have been quite an experience for Electa who had come from the rich green fields of Mercer County ordinarily watered not by irrigation ditches but by God's own rain.

Who can forget the desert sandstorms when the light of day was blocked out and tragedy struck the clothes hanging on the line? Again, an early historian gives a dramatic picture:

> The Sisters were accustomed to hail, rain, and snow storms, but they were somewhat alarmed and

fascinated when big, black clouds darkened the sky and a high wind precipitated loads of sand upon the earth. The Sisters in wonderment remained outdoors and watched the spectacle until the few scraggy bushes . . . dignified by the name of trees, and which grew a few feet away from where the Sisters were standing, were blotted from the landscape.

Hastening into the house, they were enveloped by swirling clouds of dust. They had forgotten to close doors and windows at the approach of the sandstorm. When the storm subsided, the dust somewhat settled on furniture and floors and they could again breathe, they set to work vigorously with dust pans and brooms to 'shovel' the sand from their living quarters.

Care of Homeless Children

The voices of children had been heard in the convent yard for some years before Electa arrived. From the very beginning in 1903, the sisters at St. Mary's gave their hearts to the orphaned and abandoned. The *Arizona Republic,* probably in the sixties, gave the following insights of a former homeless child given a home by the sisters:

Sister Electa was a loving mother to the children who boarded at the convent.

Mrs. Anne Beck (formerly Anne Wynn) has none of the Grade B movie recollections of living in an orphanage. She doesn't talk about stern white-aproned mistresses, thin gruel and dark-halled dormitories. Instead, happily thumbing through the pages of her memory, she paints word pictures of rope-jumping nuns, trips to the drug store for candy, and weekly games of baseball.

"One of the nuns could bat a ball clear into a neighbor's yard," Mrs. Beck said, her eyes peering past the wall as if she could still see the ball sailing off the bat. "My memories of the convent are all pleasant."

Mrs. Beck spent 15 years at St. Mary's Convent in Phoenix. She was only three, and her sister, sixteen months when their father in 1903 convinced the parish priest that he could not care for his daughters and terminally ill wife at the same time. As a result, the two little girls came to live with the nuns and six other children who were also unable to stay with their families. The only difference between the homeless children and the boarding school students was that the boarders went home in the summer and during Christmas vacation, and the orphans did not.

Mrs. Beck said she never felt like an orphan. Luckier than many of the children who were simply abandoned, Mrs. Beck said her father walked by the two-story convent at the corner of Fourth and Monroe every day on his way home from work. "We'd be upstairs, and we could hear him clear his throat and we'd go running down," she said with a broad smile. Mrs. Beck remembered one special Christmas when the nuns talked her father into playing Santa Claus.

Her days at the convent were dotted with parties, Easter egg hunts, and cotton-sock mending sessions. She said the girls' dormitory, formerly the chapel, was lined with alcoves furnished with dressers and beds. When the weather was warm, the older girls slept on a screened-in porch attached to the bedroom. Many afternoons the nuns took the children to South Mountain for picnics, and on Sundays the Wynn girls were treated by their father to band concerts on the courthouse lawn.

Mrs. Beck doesn't remember feeling frightened or alone even in her first days at the convent. "We got used to it. These sisters were very kind," she said softly. "The convent was our home. We used to go back there just like people go home to visit their mothers. My memories of my convent days were really beautiful." What a tribute to the pioneer sisters!

St. Leo's Society

After Electa had been in Phoenix five years, a Mrs. Joseph Green initiated St. Leo's Orphan and Children's Aid Society. Its purpose was to help the sisters monetarily in their efforts to rear and educate poor children of Phoenix and outlying districts. Among the members of the Society was a young boy with tuberculosis. Before he died, he gave some property on East Van Buren Street to the Society and requested that, in future years, an orphanage be built and placed under the charge of the Sisters of the Precious Blood. The title was vested in the name of the parish and, although for a time the building housed itinerant men and boys under the supervision of the Third Order of St. Francis, it was eventually sold, and the proceeds given to the sisters. The orphanage as a separate building never came about, but the sisters, under the direction of Electa, continued housing orphans in the convent.

Sisters Celesta (left) and Electa were devoted partners in the ministry for many years.

Over the years, the sisters shared their quarters as a safe haven for boys and girls from all over the country who came to the dry climate of Arizona for their health. There were also students who stayed at the convent during the week. One of these, later to become Sister Kathryn (Arnoldine) Webster, recalls that when she and her sisters arrived at the convent on Monday, they brought a five-gallon can of milk as payment for their room and board. Similarly, the sisters received countless other children over the years.

In 1942 Sister Simplicia McGreevy and Sister Regis

Kirschner, General Councilors, together with the Phoenix sisters, decided to restrict the boarders to the following categories: Catholics, elementary school children, and seventh and eighth grade girls who had previously attended a Catholic school. Boys were excluded. The sisters, ever alert to the needs of the poor, required that 10 of the 25 girls accepted be from families too poor to pay.

Boarding School Closes

Eventually, the old convent building with all its annexes was condemned as unsafe. In 1944 the sisters were finally forced to discontinue their service to orphans and boarders. The last boarder to leave was Bertha who had been brain-damaged as a baby by an abusive parent. The sisters had cared for Bertha for many years, but with the closing of the boarding school, she was taken to the Maria Joseph Home in Dayton where Precious Blood sisters cared for her lovingly until she died.

The old convent structure was razed, and a new, modern building was erected as a convent home for the sisters. Preserved, however, was the beautiful chapel around which the convent rooms were built "as two arms coming together with Jesus as the center."

With the exception of a three-year period in the thirties, Electa served as superior from 1911 until her death in 1942. Canonical limitations on the number of terms a superior could serve seem to have been suspended, perhaps because Arizona was so distant from the Motherhouse. It was a six-day trip by train to Dayton, and it was important to have a reliable presence on site. Although the telephone had been invented for some time, it was rarely used.

During one of Electa's terms of office, the Great Depression of 1929 hit. Both Kathryn Webster and Charlotte Hohlweg, a boarder at the time, recall Electa's remarkable love for the unfortunate men who came to the convent asking for food. Twelve to fifteen unemployed men a day came through the open door on the Fourth Street side. The sister cook would feed them, and they would sit right there on the steps eating a good meal.

Times were hard for the sisters also, but Electa always said, "What goes out the back door comes in the front door." In the course of time, Mother Magna asked that the door be locked for safety reasons, but that didn't stop Electa and the sisters in their concern for the poor and the hungry. Again, Mother Brunner would have been proud!

Vocations

Vocations from the West were plentiful during this time, not only to the Sisters of the Precious Blood, but also to the St. Joseph sisters, the Mercy sisters, the Immaculate Heart sisters, the Holy Name sisters, the Franciscans and others. One vocation of particular interest during Electa's time was that of our first full-blooded Indian girl, Mary Aspa, later known as Sister Mary Paschal. She was born in Yuma, Arizona in 1902 and entered the Congregation at Maria Stein at the age of 20. Sister Mary Adelaide Waltz gave us the story of her short life:

> One of the fruits of the labors of the Sisters in the West was the vocation of a full-blooded Indian girl to the life of religion. Mary Aspa's physical constitution, so well adapted to the life out-of-doors, could not cope with the restraint of cloister life. Soon after her profession, she showed signs of tuberculosis and the need of a different climate. Although she was removed as soon as possible to her native climate, she could not survive. Her death was a saintly one, and her earthly remains were laid to rest in the Community's burial plot among her relatives and friends.

Another touching story of vocations during Electa's time as superior was that of two young women, Veronica and Eva Homan. They entered the Congregation in 1923, becoming Sisters Mary Raymunda and Mary Servatia, respectively. Their mother was deceased, but their "Papa" agreed to let his two girls go all the way to Ohio to enter the convent. Tragically, they both died from consumption within six weeks of each other. "Papa" was devastated! He kept the letters his daughters had written to him, and eventually they found their way into the Archives of the Congregation.

The letters to their father have all the pious enthusiasm of young women preparing to be Brides of Christ. An early letter from Veronica says, "Eva and I are both well, and so very happy, Papa. Not a wild joy, but the peace of Christ, the peace that the world cannot give." On December 12, 1927, however, Eva wrote that Veronica had consumption and was not long for this earth. She added, "I am going to tell you the whole truth, dear Papa. I have consumption or tuberculosis too . . . [but] I shall be all right and get well." One can only imagine the sorrow that overwhelmed Electa and the Phoenix community at this double tragedy for Mr. Homan and for them. Veronica entered eternity on March 30, 1928, and Eva, on May 11 of the same year. They rest next to each other in the Maria Stein Cemetery.

The Missions

It would seem enough that the Sisters of the Precious Blood came to Arizona for the sole purpose of teaching the

Sisters pose at an Indian Mission with a heavily-laden four-footed friend.

children of St. Mary's. But from Celesta and Pancratia's "Tin Lizzie" days at the Indian Government School to outlying missions, the Precious Blood of Jesus drenched an ever-expanding area of desert sands.

One day shortly before the Christmas of 1941, Electa entered the recreation room with a mischievous look on her face. She looked around at each sister and then said, "Now sit down and hold your breath." They looked at one another wondering what she was going to tell them. Dramatically, she read the names of the sisters appointed to open three new mission fields to teach catechism. Sisters Angelita Gerlach and Eva Reichert were to go to Guadalupe; Sisters Vincentia (Frances) Ziebert and Rosalie Kastner, to Scottsdale; and Sisters Silveria (Rose Marie) Raney and Elsina (Mary Jane) Thobe, to Tin Village.

In addition to these new missions, Sisters Palmarita, Laurietta (Rita) Klosterman, and Cerona Schieltz were already serving the older mission of Tempe, and Sisters Mary John Brandewie and Dolorita (Mildred) Koewler, the mission at Mesa. Altogether, the sisters labored in five outstanding mission outposts, working to make "the Precious Blood of our Savior's five wounds fruitful on many immortal souls."

What was it like on the missions? Silveria, Vincentia, Rosalie and Elsina provided an account of their first mission experience in December 21, 1941. The four eager missionaries crowded into the back seat of a very shabby-looking car and were on their way. Ten miles later they arrived at their destination—Tin Village. The church, consisting of three walls and a tin roof studded with holes, was the center of attention. One side was open with a wire stretched across it to keep animals out. Inside was a poor weather-beaten altar with two candles and a rag for an altar cloth. A few benches without backs stood outside.

When the sisters were ready to begin instructions, they rang the old bell to summon the children. But no one showed up! Forlorn, Elsina and Silveria started walking and soon found two girls who agreed to look for others. When they rang the bell a second time, boys and girls began to assemble rather tentatively. Forty were enrolled that day!

The sisters began instructions with the Christmas story. Unfortunately, the little ones had no idea what Christmas meant. After Silveria tried her best, Elsina taught them the hymn, "O Lord, I am not Worthy." When the class was dismissed, the children disappeared until the bell was rung for Mass at nine o'clock. Electa, Pancratia and Sister Flavia Waller arrived in time for Mass, and all knelt on the dirt floor for the Holy Sacrifice. The Precious Blood poured over this desolate and forgotten part of God's world.

The Valley of the Sun is cold in December. The children were shivering since many had no coat or sweater. Promising to return with clothing, the sisters left with the smiles of all blessing them. On December 26, Electa arranged for a bus to take the sisters on a visiting tour of the missions, and all of Tin Village came out to meet them. After distributing treats and clothing to both children and adults, Celesta took the measurements of the altar, according to Electa's directions, so that she might make a new altar cloth. A chronicler of the times wrote:

> The motherly heart of dear Sister Electa being touched by the conditions of these, God's precious souls, plans a Christmas treat. On December 28 all return with oranges, candy, cookies, crackers, and popcorn. And boxes of clothing and toys! For the ladies, there are Rosaries and for the men, grapefruit. For the chapel there is a dustpan, broom, rug and a temporary altar cloth. The time comes for Mass. With the assistance of the "Majestra" (chief), children, men, and women arrive to sit on the benches the men have rounded up. Father gets out his poor little collection box. The Sisters surprise him with a new one with a handle on it. The congregation gives of its poverty and the parish is richer by a couple of dollars!

The plight of the Indians touched the hearts of the sisters. One of their reports tells us that

> . . . these poor people do not own the land on which they are living and are in danger of being chased off at any time. All last week they kept moving in farther

as the cavalry force next to them continues to expand. To them we can apply the words concerning Christ, 'They have no where to lay their heads.'

Beginning with the Government School for Indians, the Sisters of the Precious Blood brought the message of Christ's redemption to approximately 20 different missions in the Valley of the Sun. The sisters taught in tiny drafty churches, in poor little homes, and outdoors on benches, if they could find any. They taught without textbooks, blackboards, chalk, paper or pencils. They brought the message of the Saving Blood of Jesus on shivering January days and in stifling summer heat. But they got the message across, and the Valley of the Sun is richer for it.

The Yaqui Indian village of Guadalupe where the sisters from St. Mary's had taught religion on Sundays for many years was, in 1968, fortunate to welcome two resident sisters—Sisters Vera Heile and Mary Georgiana Pahl. They ministered to the bodily and spiritual needs of the impoverished Mexicans and Indians of the village. Although several sisters came at times to minister with them, Vera and Georgiana lovingly persevered in their service until 1982 when it was time sorrowfully to say, *adios*. In all the missionary activities of the sisters, motherly Electa and hundreds of sisters who served in Arizona brought Mother Brunner's love to the poor and oppressed, especially to Native American and Mexican children.

In a letter to Mother Magna Lehman, dated January 6, 1942, Electa thanked the sisters in Dayton for 140 calendars they had made for the missions in Arizona. Added to those made by the upper grades of St. Mary's, 440 calendars were distributed, reminding the Indians of Sunday Mass and Feasts of Obligation. Electa added:

> If dear Sister Acursia [Wiederkehr] could have witnessed the scene of the Rosary distribution, she would get strength enough to make hundreds of them for 1942 Christmas. . . . But, where 440 calendars are devoured (one to a family), 440 Rosaries are only a small supply for so many children. So don't

stop. We need so many. The old ladies enjoy big, highly colored Rosaries. I am wondering to myself whether dear Sister Sixta [Enneking] would be able to find one or two Altar cloths for Tin Village. Linen is very scarce here and I fear the Indians who offered to collect money among themselves . . . would get frightened if I'd tell them the price. They gave us $1.40, but we can use that for everything else they need.

Toward the close of this letter, Electa wrote, "I better stop my scribbling; it is so cold, my fingers are stiff." Nine months later those fingers that had served so many, so lovingly, would be stilled in death.

Blackouts

Toward the end of Electa's life, the United States entered World War II. The West Coast felt especially vulnerable. As superior, Electa had to plan for "blackouts" and emergencies. An early sister historian tells us that

> . . . all day she [Electa], together with Sisters Celesta, Edwina, Fidelis, Angelita and others prepared curtains, cardboard and everything that might serve to shut out all light from the outside. Perhaps one of these days we will have some kind of a drill, as we have arranged to have in school. There the children will be marched into the basement from the second floor and into the hall from the first floor. While there, the children will be engaged in saying the Rosary, ejaculations, singing songs, and anything suitable to keep them occupied. Plans have already been made for carrying on sewing classes with the 6th, 7th, and 8th grades in preparing clothing for defense. One of our city doctors will conduct First Aid Classes for the boys of the above-mentioned grades.

In the late 1950s, all the sisters in Arizona gathered at St. Mark's for a community meeting.

In a letter dated January 5, 1942, Electa commented that St. John's Mission was preparing to take in over 100 children if they must be brought in from the coast. Fortunately, this was never needed.

Fond Memories

Sisters had many fond recollections of Electa. Kathryn Webster says she was "marvelous, extraordinary. She could not hear, but could take care of everything. The sisters and the children loved her." Rita Klosterman remembers:

> . . . how very kind she was, that even though she was deaf, she understood, was quite intuitive. . . . Each evening she put out a bowl of varied kinds of fresh fruit for the sisters who were preparing lessons. On occasion she would come over to school and bring snacks, usually pastry for the sisters because she felt they might need something during the day.

Electa was a conscientious religious, but not at all straight-laced. She was understanding even about attendance at prayer. Noticing one day that Laurietta looked tired when she returned from her Saturday mission ministry, Electa suggested that she rest instead of going to prayer. This was typical of this dear superior.

Had she not possessed a deep prayer life, Electa could not have been the ever kind and generous person who graced St. Mary's for 31 years. In 1925, with Mother Agreda Sperber's approval, a chapel with air-conditioning was built so that the sisters could "spend some leisure time without risking prostration." It was to this Chapel of Our Lady of Guadalupe that Electa brought prospective postulants with their families before their departure for Dayton. For the first time, the candidate would be overwhelmed with the sisters' beautiful rendition of "Veni Sponsa Christi" [Come, Spouse of Christ].

The final "Veni Sponsa Christi" call came to Electa on October 12, 1942. Pancratia wrote an account of her last days.

Sister Electa left Phoenix on October 1 to go to Mesa. For days before, she and Sister Irma Dick were busy sewing, patching and what-not for Mesa. She remained there until October 6. That afternoon we had a rather severe sandstorm, and by the time Sister reached home after 7 p.m., she had asthma pretty bad. She forced herself the next day to remain at her desk—the statements had been piling up. On Wednesday her cheeks were flushed and she heaved quite a bit.

Pancratia goes on to say that Electa developed a high fever, bronchitis, and a heart problem. She called the doctor and asked him to tell Electa she should not go to chapel.

Veni Sponsa Christi

On October 10, Franciscan Father Brian came to Electa's bedside, and she received Viaticum, Extreme Unction and the Papal Blessing. The next day the sisters took Mother Emma's picture from the wall and gave it to her. By this time her eyes were weakened, but after a moment she recognized Mother Emma and smiled, saying, "Mother Emma! Mother Emma! She must help." After a short time she said, "Now I want Mother Brunner also!" She smiled in happiness when the sisters brought her a picture of the beloved Foundress.

The following day found her so weak that Father Brian was again called. Electa's last audible words were those of her favorite prayer, "All I have and all I am, My God, Thou gavest me; And all I have and all I am I give it back to Thee." She did not struggle. Calmly, without any outward sign, she slipped away.

Who better to come to lead Electa into the company of the "Elect" than Mother Emma and Mother Brunner? The lives of Electa, Emma and Maria Anna reflected the LOVE that Jesus poured out in His Precious Blood, once on Calvary, and over and over again on the sands of the Valley of the Sun.

*Sisters Edwina (left) and Cortona celebrate
years of service in Arizona.*

No story of the Arizona community during this period would be complete without highlighting two other sisters whose names were always connected—Sisters Edwina Glaser and Cortona Von Rohr who served a total of 109 years in Arizona.

Sister Mary Edwina

Edwina, nee Lena Glaser, left her native Dayton, Ohio for Arizona in 1911 because of her delicate health. Although doctors had told her she might have as little as two years to live, she spent 52 years—the rest of her long life there. She taught mostly seventh and eighth graders and was intensely dedicated to teaching. She spent 31 years at St. Mary's, 12 years of which she was principal. In the early years, she was considered the "mother" of the boarding school children.

Edwina helped pioneer Queen of Peace School in nearby Mesa in 1942, and stayed there 18 years. Besides her regularly assigned work in the school, she spent considerable time on the missions, especially during the summers, working with Mexican American and Indian children, always generously giving of herself to share the love of God with them.

Eventually, the years began to catch up with her. In 1960 at age 72, she moved to Tucson where she was a loving and cheerful presence to the sisters at Mother of Sorrows School. She helped the teachers in any way she could until about a year before she died. Then she was content to spend her days in prayer, reading and being present to the sisters.

Sister Virginia (DeLellis) Beene has given us an account of Edwina's last days. She entered St. Joseph Hospital in Tucson on Valentine's Day in 1963 where she stayed for 59 days. The hospital did not charge for her long stay because "her very presence was an inspiration for the young nurses and was reward enough."

While she was at the hospital, Bishop Francis J. Green of Tucson visited her each week. Before his visit during Holy Week, Edwina said to Virginia, "Pretty me up. The Bishop is coming." She wanted to wear her lace-edged bed jacket so she would look her best.

On March 19, Edwina sent for Virginia, her superior at that time. Thinking it was an emergency, Virginia rushed to the hospital. When she arrived, the elderly nun told her it was the feast of St. Joseph and she was going to die that day. She felt she needed permission to do so. Virginia replied that if God wanted her to die, she certainly had her permission and blessing.

She did not, however, die on that day. On April 12, Good Friday, her dear friend, Sister Cortona Von Rohr, and other sisters from Mesa came to visit her. She was alert and conscious during the visit. Shortly after Cortona said her last good-byes and left, Edwina slipped into a coma from which she never emerged. She died on Easter Sunday, April 14, 1963 at age 74—52 years after she had come to Phoenix in "delicate" health!

Throughout her life in Arizona, Edwina was known and appreciated for her ever-youthful enthusiasm, cheerfulness and sense of humor. Sister LaSalette Hageman, who had come to Phoenix in 1925 as a young sister in failing health, remembers Edwina as an understanding and loving principal and a great example as a religious. Edwina's deep concern for all children, especially the poor, influenced LaSalette and eventually brought her, in 1951, as teacher and principal to the struggling Mexican parish of Sacred Heart in southeast Phoenix. Father John A. Deenihan of Queen of Peace said of Edwina, "Of all the women I have known in life, I think she was the closest to God."

At her funeral Mass the Bishop's representative indicated the debt that the people of Arizona owed her:

> Men from all walks of life whom I have met in the vicinity of Phoenix and Mesa often asked, 'Do you know Sister Edwina?' The way in which they asked showed a great devotion to her indicating she had given them something they will never forget. She has left precious memories in the Diocese which will bear fruit for years to come.

Sister Mary Cortona

Like Esperanza, Cortona's first language was German. Born Lena Von Rohr in Switzerland in 1881, she came to the United States to join the Precious Blood community in 1903. After profession she taught in Botkins, Ohio for two years. Following this, she was assigned to Phoenix in 1909 to teach primary grades at St. Anthony School. She spent 17 years there touching the minds and hearts of little Mexican children with her loving and gentle ways. Cortona grew so proficient in Spanish that when St. Anthony's closed in 1926, she was transferred across the street to the high school where she taught Spanish for the next 16 years.

With Sister Mary John Brandewie and her long-time friend, Edwina, Cortona pioneered the opening of Queen of Peace School in Mesa and stayed there for the next 15 years. Once again, she taught primary grades, her first love.

Retiring from teaching in 1957 at age 76, she remained living in the convent at Queen of Peace to "keep the home fires burning" and to provide gentle services for the sisters.

On November 6, 1963, she celebrated the sixtieth anniversary of her entrance into the community. An unsigned record from that time reports, "The appearance of this fragile little Sister certainly belies her 83 years, for she manifests the same inner strength and outward capacity for action which have been hers in the past." Father Deenihan expressed his gratitude to Sister for her prayers and good works. Through her, "The Jewel in the sand," as he put it, "this parish has been especially blest."

In 1966 Cortona said good-bye to Arizona and returned to the community's retirement facility in Ohio where she spent her days "in quiet and prayer . . . still inspiring others—young sisters, nurses, and elderly companions—with her gentle cheerfulness." Never did she forget Arizona, nor did Arizona forget her. Through her, many people came to know the love of God and of her neighbor. She slept her final sleep and joined her life-long friend, Edwina, the other Lena, in 1970.

Epilogue

In the dining room of San Luis Rey Convent in California there is a wall hanging that depicts Maria Anna Brunner dispensing bread to the needy. Artist Sister Eileen Tomlinson included in her work of art the words of the foundress: "I hope to contribute to this good work even in Eternity." Maria Anna never crossed the Atlantic Ocean. She probably didn't even know about the Territory of Arizona, but through her followers, she has walked the desert sands and canyon rims of that beautiful state for almost a hundred years.

These stories have centered on the beginnings of ministry in the Valley of the Sun, that cup of gold in central Arizona embraced by the rugged arms of Camelback, Squaw Peak, Superstition and South Mountains. But Mother Brunner has poured the Precious Blood over other Arizona sands to be recounted in other stories.

Camelback Mountain overlooks the Valley of the Sun.

Responding to the educational, health and spiritual needs of God's people, Maria Anna has traveled south to Casa Grande, Tucson, Sells, Picture Rocks, Chandler, and San Luis. She has traveled westward to Hispanics in Somerton, Yuma and Kingman. She has gone north to the beautiful canyons and the colorful cliffs of Navajo land—Chinle, Fort Defiance,

Sanders, and Manuelito (New Mexico). Her presence has been felt in Holbrook, Prescott, Winslow and even in Sun City. She has lovingly embraced the poor—Indians, Mexicans and children of varying shades of white. From heaven, Maria Anna even today crimsons the sands of Arizona with Jesus' Precious Blood.

The Sisters of the Precious Blood continue to be Esperanzas of HOPE, Celestas of FAITH and Electas of LOVE as they begin their second century in Arizona in the brooding presence of Camelback Mountain.

I Come to Do Your Will

by

Helen Weber CPPS

The Story of
Ludgeria Bellinghausen CPPS
(1890-1984)

Love of Teaching

As she left the office of the Mother Superior, the tall young nun quietly pulled the door closed behind her and looked for a place to sit down. She had just received shocking news and needed time to let it sink in. After a few minutes, she composed herself with great effort and moved toward the chapel as her superior had instructed her to do.

The soft squeak of her leather shoes on the waxed terrazzo floor and the gentle swish of her habit were the only sounds breaking the silence of the long corridor leading to the chapel. After a deep genuflection before the Blessed Sacrament, she quietly slid into a pew and knelt with her head bowed. This just couldn't be right, she thought. She loved teaching and knew that she was good at it. How could she ever do what was being asked of her now?

As 36-year-old Sister Ludgeria Bellinghausen prayed for God's grace to accept her new assignment, memories of her 16 happy years of teaching at Our Lady of Good Counsel School in Cleveland, Ohio kept intruding. Faces of children passed before her: the bright and the dull, the self-confident and the fearful, lovely young girls and handsome lads. She loved them

Our Lady of Good Counsel School, Cleveland,
was the site of Ludgeria's teaching days.

103

all and delighted in their company. They could be a challenge, but more often they were a joy.

Recollections of the sights and sounds of happy children continued to bombard Ludgeria as she tried to grasp what she was now being called to do. Mother Mary Agreda Sperber (1924-36) had just informed her that she was to go to St. Gregory's Seminary, the preparatory seminary for the Archdiocese of Cincinnati, Ohio, as infirmarian for sick priests and seminarians. Ludgeria's urgent prayers ranged from "How could this be?" and "I don't want to do this," to "Please, God, help me accept this in holy obedience," and "Yes, Lord, I will do your will."

Teaching as a Novice

Ludgeria knew she had entered the Congregation to be a religious, not merely a teacher. Although she found great satisfaction in watching children under her tutelage grow and mature, she knew deep down that teaching at Good Counsel was not to be her whole life. She had come to Cleveland in 1910 as a novice after only one year of postulancy at Maria Stein Convent. Because there was a great need for teachers at that time, some novices possessing obvious potential were missioned to teach with only a rudimentary education and a promise of guidance from the principal and other sisters. At Good Counsel Ludgeria had received excellent modeling and had become an effective and confident teacher. Quietly she thanked God for the wonderful group of 25 sisters with whom she had lived there. She had been truly blessed.

Since leaving Maria Stein, Ludgeria had experienced little other than her teaching and her life with the sisters. She had become a beloved and trusted teacher, and each year she eagerly anticipated receiving her teaching assignment. Over the years, because of her versatility and willingness to do whatever she was asked, she had taught grades two through eight. She knew she had done well and had become a good teacher. Now, she was being asked to be still more versatile and make even greater adjustments in her life.

Joyful memories of blessings received mingled with bitter tears of loss and separation. After a brief period of self-pity, she blinked back her tears, straightened her shoulders, and looked up at her crucified Lord saying "Yes" to what was being asked. Once again she put her trust in God and stepped into the unknown just as she had done some 17 years earlier when she left her home and family in Missouri. As the oldest of nine children, she had learned to accept and adjust to what was being asked of her.

Early Years

Elizabeth Bellinghausen, who would receive the name of Sister Mary Ludgeria at investiture, was born in rural Halbur, Iowa on February 9, 1890. She was the first of three children born to Peter Bellinghausen and Gertrude Koenig. When Elizabeth was four years old, her father died. Her mother then married William Bellinghausen—no relation to her father. Her mother and stepfather had six children, the youngest of which was only one-year-old when Elizabeth entered the convent in 1909.

As a child, Elizabeth attended a small country school and had little contact with religious sisters. The Bellinghausen children received most of their religious education from their parents. When it was time to prepare for first reception of the sacraments of Penance and Holy Eucharist, however, the children attended the Catholic parish school about five miles from their farm home. When that time came for Elizabeth, she lived temporarily with a group of Franciscan sisters. Besides missing her family very much, she found the sisters to be "very stern and exacting." She was relieved and happy when that year was finished.

Elizabeth first met Precious Blood sisters in Templeton, Iowa where she went for Confirmation, and again later, in Montrose, Missouri when her family moved there. Though she was no longer in school at that time, having stopped at the completion of eighth grade, she observed Precious Blood sisters teaching her younger siblings. Her autobiography maintains that the sisters' demeanor drew her to the community: "The sisters were always reserved and always in Church for services. They also were kind and not rough with children."

With the blessings of her mother and stepfather, Elizabeth responded to the call to religious life and entered the Sisters of the Precious Blood along with two other young women from Missouri on August 12, 1909. She evidently did not find it difficult to adjust to community life because, as she said, "I was accustomed to the work we were asked to do." Early in life she had learned to adapt herself to the various ways work can be done.

Haven for Immigrants

Now, with God's help, Ludgeria would use her native adaptability to move from teaching to seminary work—though she knew she would sorely miss the world of Our Lady of Good Counsel. This parish had been established in 1908 primarily to assist recent immigrants, many from Eastern Europe, keep their faith strong as they adjusted to living in the United States. The Industrial Revolution was in high gear in Cleveland, and immigrants, assured of work in the newly constructed factories, flocked to the city. They begged their priests for schools to provide a Catholic environment and religious education for their children as they struggled in predominantly Protestant America. Bishops encouraged pastors to open schools; pastors, in turn, sought ways and means to obtain teaching sisters.

Late in the summer of 1908, Father Luke Rath CPPS, pastor at OLGC, sent a frantic telegram to Mother Josephine Boetsch at Maria Stein requesting that sisters be sent immediately to help him open a school in his parish. Mother Josephine, however, was not at home when the telegram arrived. In her absence, Sister Victoria Drees, directress of schools, together with the Council, assumed responsibility for committing six sisters to Good Counsel for the school year about to begin.

One can imagine Mother Josephine's shock upon her return since assignments for the school year had already been made. Nevertheless, she accepted the decision made in her absence and somehow managed to fulfill the request. School opened September 10, 1908 with 150 students. Two years later, as a novice, Ludgeria was assigned to Cleveland, just as several novices before her had been. One of the duties of Sister Genevieve Kaselka, the first principal, was to instruct and mentor novices assigned to her in the art and profession of teaching.

When Ludgeria arrived at Good Counsel, the school was already thriving. During her 16 years there, the enrollment increased to over 1000 children of 12 nationalities with a wide variety of ethnic and cultural practices and customs. OLGC exemplified American Catholic education at its best, providing access to quality education for thousands of immigrant children while, at the same time, enabling them to preserve their cultural heritage.

Throughout her long life, Ludgeria fondly remembered her years at Good Counsel. Sisters who knew Ludgeria invariably spoke of her love for teaching. They recalled her describing very large classes of 60, 70, and even 80 students, always adding that such large classes were possible only because the children had been so well-disciplined at home.

Service in Seminaries

It was with very mixed feelings that Ludgeria left her life in the classroom and made the move to St. Gregory Seminary. With the acceptance of her assignment, she entered upon a ministry which would encompass 23 years of her religious life. She served at St. Greg's for 10 years, and later, for six years at St. Thomas Seminary in Denver, Colorado. Her final seven working years were spent at Immaculate Heart Seminary in San Diego, California.

When Mother Maria Anna Brunner, foundress of the Sisters of the Precious Blood, was a young wife and mother, she passed on her great admiration and respect for priests to her children, and later, to her first followers. She rejoiced when two of her sons became priests. The Congregation's official history, *Not with Silver or Gold*, notes:

> One of the important tasks to which the first
> Sisters devoted their time . . . was the domestic work
> in the seminary founded by Father Brunner at
> Loewenberg. This practice, which fitted in with
> Mother Brunner's plan to be of utmost assistance to
> priests through prayer and personal service, became
> traditional in the Congregation (p. 333).

In keeping with this tradition, Mother Emma Nunlist in 1923 acceded to the request of Archbishop Henry Moeller of Cincinnati to send sisters to do domestic work at St. Gregory's Seminary, replacing the Sisters of Charity who had been doing this service until that time.

Ludgeria arrived at St. Greg's in the summer of 1926 and stayed for the next ten years. In addition to being infirmarian, she was given charge of supervising workers at the seminary, and for the last six years, she was superior of the sisters. Growing up in rural Iowa as the oldest child in a family of nine children, she undoubtedly had learned how to take care of minor injuries and illnesses. Was that enough to qualify her as infirmarian at St Gregory's? Blindly going where she was told, always trusting in God's grace and the help of others, was becoming a guiding principle in her life.

St. Gregory's Seminary

After a period of adjustment to life away from the classroom, Ludgeria delighted in her work with the seminarians. They were high school students, not much different from the boys she had taught and trained as servers at Our Lady of Good Counsel. Another of her responsibilities was to direct the work of young women hired to clean, do laundry, work in the kitchen or serve table. Her kindness, her gentle but firm ways, and her fairness created a pleasant working environment.

At 36, Ludgeria began a new ministry at St. Gregory's Seminary in Cincinnati.

As the years went by, Ludgeria endeared herself to students and to priest faculty members as well. Respected by both, she often found herself caught between them. Two stories from that time illustrate this. Seminarians were not allowed to have personal radios which were becoming popular about 1930. Of course, many students did have radios, but kept them hidden. On her autobiographical tape, Ludgeria relates the following:

The boys were not allowed to have radios, but they kept them in a can behind the door with the mop. One boy had a larger one and asked me to keep it on the third floor where the vestments were. As he was carrying the heavy box up the stairs, he was met by a priest who asked him what be was carrying and was told to open it.

"Where do you think you are going?"

"Up to the vestment room."

"Does Sister Ludgeria know this?"

"Yes, she does."

Later I was told that Father Pettigrew, the rector, wanted to see me. I was never afraid of him; he was always respectful.

"Do you know that the boys are keeping their radios up in the vestment room?"

"Yes."

"You never told me!"

"Did you want me to?"

"No."

Another story:

> *I had charge of the infirmary and was very careful about the beds. The boys were never allowed to be on them. I saw a pillow that looked big and not the way I had left it. I took the corner and shook it; out came a radio—a good one. The boy said,*
> *"How could you?"*
> *"You should have put a sign on it: 'Do Not Shake Me. Radio Inside.'"*
> *"You won't squeal on me?"*
> *I never squealed on them. I told the student:*
> *"We have a disciplinarian here, and it is his job to check, not mine."*

Life at St. Gregory Seminary was very pleasant for Ludgeria. She enjoyed the work; both priests and students respected her. She was a generous and gracious superior to the sisters. Then in the summer of 1936, at the age of 46, her life took another radical turn. At the Congregation's General Chapter, the delegates chose her to be a member of newly-elected Mother Magna Lehman's Council.

Ludgeria's duties as Councilor did not require her to live at the Dayton Motherhouse. In addition to serving on the General Council, she was also appointed bookkeeper at Kneipp Springs Sanitarium near Rome City, Indiana. According to her own telling, when she received this assignment, she did not even know how to write a check

Kneipp Springs—Background

Tucked in among the rolling hills above Sylvan Lake in Noble County, an old and dilapidated building calling for renovation came to the attention of the Sisters of the Precious Blood. Kneipp Sanitarium had been built and managed by Doctor William Geiermann, an enthusiastic hydrotherapeutist. He firmly believed in the curative effects of water for treating people with physical and emotional tension. He was convinced that the natural beauty of the lake country of northeastern Indiana was a perfect spot for his sanitarium. However, by 1901 he was financially unable to carry on his work. He was searching for the right people to purchase this property and continue what he had begun.

About this same time, Mother Emma Nunlist came to the sanitarium to receive the "Kneipp treatment" to ease tensions stemming from her responsibilities in the Congregation. Water

Kneipp Springs Sanitarium in NE Indiana was
Ludgeria's third mission.

therapy—consisting of baths, spraying of water forces on the body, and resting in wet blankets—was a major component of the treatment. Also included was a regulated diet along with various herbal teas. In the summer time, patients were encouraged to wade in the outdoor pools or to swim in the cold waters of Sylvan Lake. The value of such water treatments had been well established in the previous century in Europe where they were popularized by Monsignor Sebastian Kneipp, whose name became connected with them.

$25,000 Purchase

One can assume that during the time of her treatments, Dr. Geiermann spoke to Mother Emma about his desire to sell the property. In the fall of 1901 she returned to the sanitarium with Mother Ludovica Scharf, a member of her Council, and Sister Margaret Schlachter, who had studied the Kneipp treatments in Europe under the direction of Msgr. Kneipp. Although the buildings needed a great amount of repair, and renovations were critical, the sisters agreed that the location was ideal for a health resort. The Council determined that the Congregation would purchase the buildings and the eighty acres of wooded groves with rich mineral springs and small lakes for $25,000. The Archbishop of Cincinnati, William Henry Elder, gave his blessing to this new ministerial endeavor. Sister Margaret was named the first administrator, and Sister Agreda Sperber, treasurer.

Under the excellent leadership of Margaret and Agreda, Kneipp Springs blossomed and thousands of people came for the water treatments and for the atmosphere of prayer and quiet provided by the sisters. Guests could attend daily Mass and share in the sisters' special privilege of perpetual adoration of the Blessed Sacrament. When Agreda was elected Mother Superior in 1924, she handed over a financially sound and effective institution to her successor, Sister Rogata Ruth.

After her 12-year term as Mother Superior, Mother Agreda returned to Kneipp Springs as local superior in 1936. The world was in the depths of economic depression. The number of guests had decreased substantially over the past six years, but, thanks to the frugality of the sisters, the sanitarium was able to continue without being a financial burden to the Congregation. This was due largely to the abundance of home-grown fruits and vegetables, as well as home butchering for meat. In fact, the institution was a source of money to help support other ministries of the community.

Ludgeria Arrives

It was at this time that Ludgeria arrived at the Springs. Having had no training or experience in financial or administrative matters, she was fortunate to be under the direct and able guidance of Mother Agreda. In 1938, however, Mother Agreda died, and Rogata completed her term as superior. In 1942 Ludgeria was appointed superior and administrator of Kneipp Springs.

Since Ludgeria had served from 1936 to 1942 on the General Council of the Congregation in addition to her work at Rome City, she was well aware of both the value of the ministry and its needs. She accepted the appointment with determination to build on what her predecessors had accomplished and to contribute toward further development and progress.

Relying upon her native intelligence and strong work ethic, Ludgeria honed her administrative skills at Kneipp Springs. She took on a wide variety of tasks with her customary good humor and sense of responsibility. Her custom was to face immediate problems head on, taking care of them one day at a time, using all means at her disposal to bring about effective solutions.

Ludgeria motivated sisters and lay employees with great warmth, inspiring them to do their very best. She was encouraging, but she could also be demanding. Believing firmly that hard work could accomplish anything, she expected concerted effort from everyone. Always kind and generous, however, she never asked of others what she herself was not willing to do.

State Inspections

Ludgeria's work at Kneipp Springs was especially challenging because of the changing times. Health care institutions had come under scrutiny by State Departments. To reflect better the nature of the place, the name of the sanitarium was changed to Kneipp Springs Health Spa. More than just a name change, this also meant a new classification. Regular state inspections would now be mandatory.

A great challenge for Ludgeria was to get Kneipp Springs licensed as a "Specialized Hospital" with all the accompanying rights and privileges. This required extensive renovation,

Ludgeria provided leadership at Kneipp Springs for 15 years.

including nurse call and fire protection systems, increased water capacity, fire escapes and sprinkling systems. The licensing also necessitated new and expensive refrigeration units for preservation of food.

The greatest change required by state inspections was that home-grown foods could no longer be served to guests. Food now had to be purchased from food companies whose products were state certified. No longer could gardens, orchards, and cattle be used for the delicious, plentiful and nutritious meals for which Kneipp Springs had become famous. This change precipitated future financial problems for Kneipp Springs and for the Congregation, but not until long after Ludgeria's departure.

1946 Auction

During a period of renovations in February of 1946, the sisters at the Springs decided to help raise money by auctioning many no-longer-needed beds, dressers, chairs and pewterware pieces stored in the attic. Excerpts from a letter to Mother Magna written by Ludgeria on the day after the auction provide an account of this event:

> *'Tis the day after the famous auction at Kneipp Springs. The day before the auction was balmy—just like a day in spring. . . . The radio announced that rain would fall that night. We urged the Sisters to pray to good St. Joseph that he keep the rain away. The yard was littered*

with things to be sold. . . . St. Joseph managed to keep the rain away. However he managed the affair in his own way, causing us hours of anxiety. . . .

The morning of the Auction Day dawned gray and bleak. . . . No rain had fallen. When we emerged from chapel, fine snow sifted downwards and, as the morning advanced, the flakes increased in size and intensity. The furniture out in the yard took on an appearance of upholstery in immaculate white. We were continuing our prayers to the dear Saint, telling him that we were grateful that it hadn't rained, but we had serious misgivings. . . .

From all accounts the auction was a success. The attic was emptied, and there was money for the continuing needs of the institution. In fact, one of the local people said that if the day had been bright and sunny, the farmers would not have felt free to go to the auction. Ludgeria ends the letter with *"So all in all, we are happy and very, very grateful to dear St. Joseph."*

Postwar Growth

In the affluent era following World War II, the number of guests at the Spa increased to about 2000 annually. With the increased income, Ludgeria renovated, remodeled and refurbished guests' rooms and redecorated chapel. But, according to her account, her greatest achievement was not in the material and financial assets or in the increased number of guests secured, but in the prestige gained through membership in various hospital associations and in being licensed. The Kneipp Springs Health Spa became known and recognized as a successful healthcare institution, and the sisters, as qualified healthcare professionals.

Never merely a business-minded administrator, Ludgeria was also superior for sisters who worked there year round and for teaching sisters who helped out in summer. Her personal file contains cards and notes from the summer sisters expressing genuine appreciation for the spirit she brought to their lives during the summer months. One sister offers her impression of Ludgeria from this time:

As a young sister, I was sent to Rome City during summer vacation to help in the kitchen. Ludgeria was very welcoming, and daily during recreation she asked me what I did to keep myself busy. . . . She'd always comment with a smile on how I was progressing! She made me feel very special and loved. . . .

Another tribute from this time follows:

Sister Ludgeria was a hard worker and a good manager. She had a warm, kind, pleasant, patient, and understanding personality which endeared her to the guests, sisters and employees. She had a dry sense of humor. She was prayerful and gave every evidence of being a happy, dedicated religious.

But once again, at the peak of her success, Ludgeria received a call from the Congregation to leave this work and use her skills and talents in yet another ministry. In the summer of 1951, she was told to pack her bags and say good-bye to her friends and colleagues. She was to leave the rolling hills of northern Indiana and head for the Rocky Mountains in Colorado.

St. Thomas Seminary

With the large influx of novices in the early 1950s, the Congregation was growing rapidly. Mother Nathalia Smith (1948-54) was thus able to respond to some of the many entreaties for sisters to serve in various ministries all over the country. One of these requests was for sisters to serve in the dietary and homemaking departments of St. Thomas Seminary in Denver, Colorado. Since the Sisters of the Precious Blood had been in Denver as homemakers in the residence of Archbishop Urban J. Vehr since 1931, and in the teaching ministry at Christ the King Parish School since 1949, Mother Nathalia agreed to send sisters.

St. Thomas Seminary was the major seminary for the Dioceses of Denver and Pueblo in Colorado and Cheyenne in

Wyoming. It had come into existence in 1907 under the leadership of Bishop Nicholas Matz, the second Bishop of Denver. Located on a 60-acre plot in the south-eastern section of Denver, it was set on a high plateau amid trees and spacious lawns with a panoramic view of the Front Range of the Rockies.

For many years after its beginning, St Thomas remained a very small school with only about 20 students. However, in the late 1920s, the Vincentians who staffed the school informed Bishop Henry Tihen that they would withdraw if St. Thomas did not become a "real" seminary. A massive recruitment and building program followed, and by the time Ludgeria arrived in 1951, enrollment had increased to about 200.

Problems with Food Service

There is no record of the early food service at the seminary, but by the 1940s, it had become a major problem for both the seminarians and the leadership of the seminary. Monsignor James Rasby, a seminarian at that time, describes how the seminary hired its cooks:

> The proctor would go down to Larimer Street (at that time the 'skid row' of Denver) and hire men off the street to come and cook. There was a revolving door of cooks. During the year before the sisters came, we had at least ten people acting as cooks. As you can imagine, the food was very bad and the kitchen, extremely dirty.

After a sufficient number of complaints, and perhaps seminarians threatening to leave, Archbishop Vehr stepped in. He had come to Colorado from Cincinnati where he had served as rector of St. Gregory Seminary during Ludgeria's years there, and he knew the Congregation well. He used his influence with Mother Nathalia to obtain sisters for St. Thomas. Before the sisters arrived, he insisted that the seminary build a new convent for them. Aware that he was seeking sisters to do hard domestic work, he showed his respect and concern for them by assuring Mother Nathalia that the

117

sisters would have good living accommodations. The new convent was blessed December 11, 1949, and the first sisters came the following summer.

*Ludgeria spent many happy days at the
Saint Thomas Seminary in Denver.*

Sister Boniface Halsema was superior of the first group of four sisters who came to Denver in 1950. After only a short time, however, Boniface became ill and returned to Dayton. Sister M. Leonides Piekenbrock filled in for a few months until a new superior could be appointed. Superiors faced the problem of whom to send to this new mission in Denver. Looking for someone both with experience in seminary work and as a local superior, they found the right combination in Ludgeria.

Once again, Ludgeria was asked to begin a new ministry. At age 61, she may not have felt as dejected as she had when asked to give up teaching at age 36. Nevertheless, after 15 years at Kneipp Springs, she surely felt the pain of separation from community, friends and colleagues.

Arrival in Colorado

After the long train ride through the rolling agricultural land of Illinois and Iowa, across miles of monotonous plains in Nebraska, Kansas and eastern Colorado, Ludgeria had her first glimpse of the Rocky Mountains. She and her companions, Sisters Christella (Alice) Heckman and Lelia (Eva) Roehrich, were met by Sisters Othilea (Elizabeth) Uhlenhake and Mechtildis (Mary Rita) Fullenkamp, both of whom had come a year earlier.

Ludgeria, facing another challenge in her life, realized it was important to establish seminary ministry as one of service, but not subservience. She was well aware that too often sisters in this kind of work were taken for granted. She believed that if the sisters would provide good and nourishing meals in an atmosphere of loving service, they could create in priests and seminarians an awareness of the ministry and value of women religious.

While always maintaining a respectful reserve, Ludgeria established a tone of attentiveness and friendliness with students and faculty. Msgr. Rasby said she brought a feeling of warmth to the seminary making it seem more of a home. He noted that she and the sisters added a spirit of festivity to holidays by preparing special foods and dining room decorations.

A Gentle Leader

Sisters serving at the seminary with Ludgeria experienced her as a gentle but exacting leader. Always a hard worker herself, she expected others to be diligent, also. She seemed to have a special gift for knowing exactly what each sister needed and for being able to provide it for her. "She was always positive and encouraging," one sister remarked. "She didn't scold you. Rather, she lifted you up and kept you going."

Sisters who worked with her in those days universally speak of her ability to work hard, but to enjoy recreation as well. Sisters Alma Catherine Huelscamp and Eva Roehrich shared stories of the fun sisters had after long days of work in the seminary kitchen. They tell of one Halloween when they had planned to frighten Ludgeria only to be frightened by her instead. Always one step ahead of them, her deep chuckle often lessened the tensions of the day.

Many of the sisters assigned to the Denver seminary with Ludgeria were young and inexperienced. She felt a keen obligation to teach them and to give them a solid start in ministry and in religious life. Marie Weber Lubeley, formerly Sister Louis Therese, came to St. Thomas directly from the novitiate. Many years later she reflected on the way Ludgeria influenced her work habits and her life:

> Sister Ludgeria spent her whole life . . . providing many different forms of service through hard work. Her convictions were strongly influenced by a hard-work ethic. Her measurements of a person's worth were related to how much that person could do and how quickly she could do it well. This philosophy was emphasized in kitchen assignments, as well as through conversation and religious direction. As a young inexperienced person, I received a lot of all three. This orientation to the working world has never left me. To this day I find that I need to account for every minute. I cannot tolerate time wasted or inefficient use of time and talents. This has been both a benefit and a drawback. I appreciate Sister Ludgeria for her role in a formation that has allowed me much success over a 45-year career.

With the opening of Cure'd Ars School in Denver in 1954, Ludgeria invited sisters assigned there to live at the seminary until their convent was completed. Sister Carmen Voisard, the first principal at the new school, tells about the great hospitality provided at the seminary. Carmen relates that Ludgeria enjoyed hearing all the details of the school world and the antics of the students, even though by that time it had been over 30 years since her days in the classroom. She willingly assisted the teaching sisters in correcting students' papers and enjoyed sharing her teaching experiences with them. It was evident that her first love of teaching had not lessened with the passing years.

Later Years in Ministry

After six years as superior at St. Thomas, Ludgeria was asked in 1957 to move to another position of leadership within a local community. When she had said her good-byes to her friends at the seminary, she took a last stroll to the west side of the grounds and gazed upon the majestic Rockies. She would soon be leaving the mountains of Colorado for the City of Seven Hills, Cincinnati, Ohio, where 21 years ago she had served at St. Gregory's Seminary.

She was assigned to St. Peter in Chains Cathedral in downtown Cincinnati as housekeeper in the rectory and superior of the sisters. Plans to restore the original cathedral, St. Peter in Chains, had been inaugurated by Archbishop Karl J. Alter (1950-69). The restored structure would replace St. Monica's Church in the suburb of Clifton as the Archdiocesan cathedral. The Archbishop projected having sisters serve as

*Ludgeria is fondly remembered as a
firm but gentle leader.*

121

housekeepers in the Cathedral residence and included accommodations for them in the renovation project.

Even before the rededication of the Cathedral in 1957,
Auxiliary Bishop Clarence G. Issenmann and several priests took
up residence there. Mother Aquinas Stadtherr (1954-66) responded positively to the request from Archbishop Alter for sisters to
serve as cooks, housekeepers and sacristan. The first four sisters—Mary Celsa (Madonna) Kempf, Mary Ephrem (Mildred)
Neuzil, Mary Aengus (Margaret) Daniels—and Janet Grieve,
took up their duties in 1956.

The sisters found working conditions at the Cathedral to
be very difficult. Within a year, Ludgeria, with her wide experience and gentle leadership style, was called upon to bring
peace, order and stability to the ministry. Providing housekeeping services for men set in their ways was more difficult
than serving seminarians, but under Ludgeria's guidance, the
sisters were able to accomplish this. She completed her term of
six years as superior in 1963. She was then 73 years old, long
past the accepted retirement age.

San Diego, California

But Ludgeria was different from most people, and she
accepted a new assignment and another term as superior for
sisters serving in a seminary. This time she found herself in
sunny Southern California at St. Francis (later, Immaculate
Heart) Seminary, one of the last missions Mother Nathalia
accepted during her term as Mother Superior. The Sisters of
the Precious Blood in 1953 had assumed responsibilities for
the dietary department in the San Diego Diocesan Seminary
in El Cajon, California, a suburb of San Diego. In 1957 the
seminary was moved to the campus of the University of San
Diego.

When Ludgeria took up her responsibilities in 1963, the
seminary was located on a magnificent piece of land on a
hilltop providing a 360-degree view. Homes and buildings
with sun-bleached stucco walls and red-tiled roofs typical of
Spanish architecture dotted the hills surrounding the property. To the east, purple-tinted mountains loomed; the sparkling

waters of San Diego Bay lay to the west. Since the sisters occupied the top floor of the seminary building, the impressive view of all this beauty was their daily gift and the envy of many. Under Ludgeria's leadership, the sisters were generous in sharing their home with its enviable view with sisters who studied at the University of San Diego and with others.

Work at the seminary was extremely demanding. Bishop Charles Buddy (1936-66) entertained extensively, frequently hosting huge banquets. Though seminarians served as waiters and dishwashers at these events, the sisters were responsible for all the cooking. In addition, the sisters were housekeepers for the priests, cleaning their living quarters and doing their laundry. Easing the burden of their hard work, Ludgeria brought her gifts of gentleness and care to the sisters. She also used her considerable skills in negotiating with priests to ensure that the sisters were seen as co-ministers in formation work at the seminary.

Praise from Sisters

Sister Lucille Rotanzi, who lived with Ludgeria in San Diego reflected:

> Living with dear Sister Ludgeria from 1963-1970 was a delightful experience. Her sense of humor was refreshing. She was such a loving person, always concerned about others. If someone was in trouble, Sister knew just what to say to encourage and console her. The seminarians felt very close to her—she inspired confidence and courage.

Sister Clara VanDeBueken recalls:

> Ludgeria was always cleaning; she even took a dust cloth to retreat, or wherever, to make sure it was clean. We told her in fun that we'd put a dust cloth in her coffin. . . . Ludgeria was like a spiritual guide for the seminarians and priests; she was a very spiritual person.

"When we asked for articles we needed," adds Sister Gladys Marie Lowe, "she gave us two pairs of shoe strings, two tooth brushes, etc., instead of one."

Visitors also appreciated Ludgeria's gentle and loving personality. Sister Eleanor McNally, former director of the Western Region, says "She was the most comforting, upbeat, positive person. Her love for and acceptance of people was remarkable." Sister JoAnn Thomas, a summer student at Immaculate Heart College living at the seminary, describes Ludgeria as "older and walking with a cane," but remembers how sensitive to a sister's need she always was, so much so that it seemed she could "smell a need."

Ludgeria celebrated her sixtieth anniversary in the Congregation while she was at Immaculate Heart. The seminarians presented her with a huge stuffed red dog which she proudly displayed. On another anniversary she received a particularly beautiful blooming plant from her admirers among the seminarians and faculty. After having the plant in her room for a day or two, one of the sisters suggested that she put the plant in chapel. She had done this on other occasions saying, "Take it to chapel for Jesus to see." This time Ludgeria responded, "He can see it here!"

Declining Health

During her years at Immaculate Heart, Ludgeria's health declined. She was hospitalized several times, once for colon cancer from which she recovered after surgery which removed about 21 inches of her intestine. After that she was not able to work a full day as she had been doing for so long. She began to think about retiring to the Congregation's retirement facility in Dayton, Ohio.

Her plans to retire were delayed, however, when Father John R. Quinn, prefect of the seminarians and later Archbishop of San Francisco, prevailed upon Ludgeria to stay longer. He cited her good example and the influence she had with the young men. She agreed to stay on, but only for one more year. She was then 80 years of age and had been serving in various ministries for 57 years.

During her seven years in Southern California, Ludgeria had made a difference in the lives of many. Priests and future priests had benefited from her wisdom, good sense and gentle caring. This elderly nun had helped to make them better men and better priests.

This time, as she left her ministry, she knew the time had come for retirement. As the plane taking her to Dayton flew over beautiful San Diego Bay, she reflected on her many years of hard work in the service of others. She prayed that she had always responded generously no matter where God called her.

Retirement

At 11:00 pm, on Monday, September 14, 1970, a TWA flight landed at Dayton International Airport bringing Ludgeria to her last place of residency, Emma Hall. With her companion, Sister Katie Lett, she arrived, tired, but happy to be back on solid ground. The C.PP.S Dialog, October, 1970 gives an account of her early days of retirement:

> After many years spent in directing domestic work in seminaries served by the community, Sister Ludgeria was ready to retire from active duty. She knew that she was leaving the beauty and dignity and warmth and friendliness of the seminary in San Diego where she worked for the last few years. . . . What she wondered about as she winged her way east was just what she would do and how she would live in retirement at Emma Hall.

Sister Mary Leonita Westerheide, coordinator of Emma Hall and superior of the sisters, welcomed Ludgeria and gave her an orientation into the services, expectations and routines of the retirement home. Very soon Ludgeria was busy renewing acquaintances with sisters she had known as novices 60 years ago and with ministry colleagues of the intervening years. Stories of their ministerial and life journeys provided hours of contented discussions. In 1970 she didn't know that she would be spending the final 14 years of her life right there in Emma Hall.

Time for Prayer

Life as a retired sister provided Ludgeria with time for the intensive, prolonged prayer which her busy life had never afforded her. She now had plenty of time to pray, to meditate and to just "be" in the presence of the Blessed Sacrament. Ludgeria's physical health and mental capacity were good during her early years in retirement. The staff remembers that she was a cooperative and active member of the Emma Hall community. She participated in house meetings, birthday parties, and fulfilled her small work responsibilities. She faithfully attended daily Eucharist and the praying of the Office. When the staff couldn't find her in her room, they soon learned that she could be found in chapel, engrossed in prayer.

Evidence of her influence on myriads of persons whose lives she had touched during her long years of ministry is found in the cards, letters, gifts and visitors she received during her retirement. Sisters she had worked with, especially her dear friend, Sister Lucille; priests she had served; and numerous lay persons she had befriended wanted to be remembered to and by this elderly nun. She was especially honored on August 15, the anniversary of her profession, and on the feasts of Christmas and Easter. One Christmas she received a large poinsettia accompanied by the following note:

> Congratulations to you, dear Sister Ludgeria, whom I deeply admire. You were a real inspiration to me. I'll always be grateful to you for your wisdom and the good advice you gave me when we were together at the Seminary in San Diego. You were

always so approachable and understanding to us all. What a gift you were to so many!

Gratefully in Prayer,
John R. Quinn
Archbishop of San Francisco

The End Nears

Ludgeria's health gradually deteriorated. No longer the tall and impressive woman she had been, she was now small and frail. A broken hip at the age of 90 was the beginning of the end for her. Sister Virginia Beene, coordinator of Emma Hall during these years, recalls:

Later when her mind had weakened and she no longer went to Mass but received Eucharist in her bedroom, she would talk to Jesus aloud. Some of the aides stood outside her room to listen to her thanksgiving after Communion. They then understood why she never complained and was never demanding. She gave a real witness to Precious Blood spirituality.

For several years before her death, Ludgeria needed to be restrained in a chair during the day so she wouldn't wander off or fall and injure herself. Just as she had always done what was asked of her, she accepted this indignity without complaint. When sisters visited her, she often enjoyed lucid moments when she could recall names and incidents. At other times she would just smile and nod.

Ludgeria's generous life came to an end on December 4, 1984. The day before her death, a doctor diagnosed her with double pneumonia. The next morning Sister Luella Huelscamp, coordinator of Emma Hall, gave her a small particle of a host and some water. She thanked Luella for bringing Holy Communion, and Luella left her to attend Mass. A short time later, Luella was called out of chapel because Ludgeria had died. She had quietly slipped away.

A great woman who had been surrounded by so many people in her life and ministry died alone, at peace with all. As she faced death, one can imagine that she obediently said, "Yes, I'm coming," as she had done so many times before. Willingly, she went into the unknown as she had spent a lifetime doing—trusting in her God.

Always a Teacher

Ludgeria, who accepted her assignment to give up teaching, never quit teaching. She was a teacher to all with whom she came in contact. She taught sisters who lived and worked with her how to be faithful stewards of time and talents. She showed lay people at Kneipp Springs ways to let go of tensions and relax in the present. She helped seminarians and priests appreciate how women religious could enhance their ministry.

But this teacher was also an able student. Ludgeria learned on the job how to be an infirmarian, how to keep books, and how to provide spiritual leadership to the sisters. She is remembered, not so much for what she did, but for the person she was in the lives of others. Her obituary described her with that wonderful phrase, "She is the kind of a person who lifted you up and kept you going."

Sources

Sources for these three biographies include:

❖ personal writings;
❖ archival material;
❖ written and oral testimony of persons who knew the subjects;
❖ interviews taped by Sister Florentine Gregory;
❖ historical and geographical background.

Biblical quotations have been taken from the Saint Joseph Edition of the New American Bible.

The photographs on pages 31, 75, 97 and 118 were taken by Helen Weber CPPS; the rest are from the Archives of the Sisters of the Precious Blood, Dayton, Ohio.

To obtain copies of this book, or of Volume I, contact:

Sisters of the Precious Blood
4000 Denlinger Road
Dayton, OH 45426

((937) 837-3302
Srs.CPPS@spbdo.com

Volume III of this series, *The Legacy Continues . . .*, will be
available in the summer of 2002.